gettyimages

1900s

Decades of the 20th Century
Dekaden des 20. Jahrhunderts
Décennies du XXe siècle

Nick Yapp

KÖNEMANN

This edition ©KÖNEMANN*, an imprint of Tandem Verlag GmbH, Königswinter
Photographs ©2001 Getty Images

This book was produced by Getty Images
Unique House, 21–31 Woodfield Road, London W9 2BA

For KÖNEMANN*:
Managing editor: Sally Bald
Project editors: Lucile Bas, Meike Hilbring
German translation: Anne Marks
French translation: Ella Lewandowsky

For Getty Images:
Art director: Michael Rand
Design: B+B
Picture editor: Ali Khoja
Editor: Richard Collins
Proof reader: Elisabeth Ihre
Editorial assistance: Tom Worsley
Special thanks: Tea McAleer

*KÖNEMANN is a registered trademark of Tandem Verlag GmbH

Printed in Germany

ISBN 3-8331-1077-5

10 9 8 7 6 5 4 3 2 1
X IX VIII VII VI V IV III II I

Frontispiece: The sun shines on Edwardian society. The proud and the fashionable
arrive at Henley railway station for the annual regatta, 4 June 1905. The London
Season was at its height – ahead lay weeks of washing and ironing for the domestics.

Frontispiz: Die Sonne scheint auf die Edwardianische Gesellschaft. Die vornehmen
Leute bei ihrer Ankunft am Bahnhof von Henley zur jährlichen Regatta, 4. Juni 1905.
Die Londoner Saison hatte ihren Höhepunkt erreicht – Berge von Wäsche und
Bügelarbeit standen dem Hauspersonal bevor.

Frontispiece : Le soleil brille sur le règne d'Édouard VII. Les membres de la belle
société arrivent en gare de Henley pour la régate annuelle, 4 juin 1905. La saison
londonienne était alors à son apogée ... et les domestiques avaient en perspective des
semaines de lessive et de repassage.

Contents / Inhalt / Sommaire

Introduction

The last sprint to the finishing line of the 19th century produced a host of inventions and innovations to launch the 20th century on its mad and merry way. There was the telephone, the telegraph, the automobile, cinematography, the X-ray, the discovery of radioactivity, the gramophone, synthetic fibres, the cathode ray, the steam turbine and a thousand other wonders, all products of the 1890s. The vocabulary, as well as the quality, of life changed almost beyond measure.

The great work on hand was rivalry – commercial, military, technical and scientific. The great powers of Europe were the most concerned. Their rivalry encompassed the globe. France, Germany and Britain measured each other's industrial might and devoted vast resources to catching up with the others or maintaining their lead. Imperial Russia watched with concern, but had trouble enough controlling its own population. The United States begged to be left alone, while seizing the chance to tighten its grip on Central America.

Away from the laboratory or the parade ground, the shipyard or the factory bench, the move to frivolity continued. Crowds flocked to music-halls, cabarets, vaudeville theatres, dance floors, movie parlours and cafés. A glass of wine or beer and a cheap cigar gave Everyman a chance to feel like a Rockefeller. Women took up smoking and drinking in public, and every kind of sport. They learnt how to drive a car and how not to have babies – though the former skill was more easily attained.

The rich dashed from one exciting event to another – the opera, the races, regattas, balls, shoots, foxhunts, presentations at Court – for the royal trade union still had many paid-up members. The poor staggered from slum to sweatshop and back again, though their own trade unions were slowly winning the struggle for better wages, shorter working hours, and safety at work. All over the world suffragettes fought for the right to vote. In a few places they were successful. Immigrants to the United States continued to pour into Ellis Island, seeking new life, new liberty, new hope. In a few cases they were successful.

And so into the brand new century. Subways were opened in New York and Paris. There was a new oil company called Standard Oil, a new disposable razor marketed by Mr Gillette, a new power source called a 'battery' made by Thomas Edison, a new automobile manufacturing company owned by Henry Ford. It was the decade of the first World Series (baseball), the first Tour de France (cycling) and the first Nobel prizes; of art nouveau and the Brownie camera; of the *Potemkin* mutiny and the San Francisco earthquake; of Pavlov's dogs and Charles Dana Gibson's 'Girls'.

The Wright brothers flew a heavier-than-air machine across the sands of Kitty Hawk, North Carolina, and Louis Blériot piloted the first plane to cross the Channel. Britain, it was said, was no longer an island. Did it matter? There was a new alliance between France and Britain – the Entente Cordiale – a pledge of help and friendship between two hitherto perennial foes. Better means of communication promised greater understanding between nations. But, as the next decade was to prove, old grudges ran deep…

Einführung

Der Endspurt des 19. Jahrhunderts brachte mit einer Flut von Erfindungen und Neuerungen das 20. Jahrhundert auf einen verrückten und heiteren Weg. Erfindungen der neunziger Jahre des letzten Jahrhunderts waren das Telefon, der Telegraf, das Automobil, die Kinematografie, der Röntgenstrahl, die Entdeckung der Radioaktivität, das Grammofon, Kunstfasern, der Kathodenstrahl, die Dampfturbine und noch viele weitere wundersame Erfindungen. Die Alltagssprache wie auch die Lebensqualität veränderten sich enorm.

Die anstehende Aufgabe war der Wettbewerb – im Handel, auf militärischem, technischem und wissenschaftlichem Gebiet. Die Großmächte in Europa waren am meisten betroffen. Sie traten rund um den Globus miteinander in Konkurrenz. Frankreich, Deutschland und Großbritannien maßen ihre Kräfte auf dem industriellen Sektor und verwendeten enorme Mittel darauf, mit der Entwicklung Schritt zu halten und ihre Vormachtstellung zu behaupten. Das russische Zarenreich beobachtete dies mit großer Sorge. Es hatte jedoch Mühe, seine eigene Bevölkerung unter Kontrolle zu halten. Die Vereinigten Staaten erlaubten sich einen Alleingang und ergriffen die Gelegenheit, den Druck auf Mittelamerika zu verstärken.

Fernab der Labors und der Exerzierplätze, der Werften und der Werkbänke setzte sich der Übermut fort. Die Menschen strömten in Konzerte, Kabaretts, Varietés, gingen zum Tanzen, ins Kino und ins Café. Mit einem Glas Wein oder Bier und einer erschwinglichen Zigarre in der Hand konnte sich jedermann wie Rockefeller fühlen. Frauen fingen an, in der Öffentlichkeit zu rauchen und Alkohol zu trinken und trieben jede Art von Sport. Sie lernten das Autofahren und zu verhüten – ersteres wurde jedoch leichter verstanden.

Die Reichen stürzten sich von einem Abenteuer in das nächste – Opern, Rennen, Regatten, Bälle, Jagden und Fuchsjagden, Einführungen am Hofe –, denn die königliche Gefolgschaft hatte noch immer viele vollwertige Mitglieder. Die Armen pendelten von den

Elendsvierteln zu den Ausbeuterbetrieben und wieder zurück, doch ihre Gewerkschaften gewannen langsam aber sicher den Kampf um höhere Löhne, kürzere Arbeitszeiten und mehr Sicherheit am Arbeitsplatz. Überall auf der Welt kämpften Frauenrechtlerinnen für das Wahlrecht. An einigen Orten waren sie erfolgreich. Nach wie vor kamen Scharen von Einwanderern in die Vereinigten Staaten nach Ellis Island und suchten dort nach einem neuen Leben, neuer Freiheit und neuer Hoffnung. Selten hatten sie dabei Erfolg.

So begann das neue Jahrhundert. In New York und Paris wurden U-Bahnen eingeweiht. Ein Erdölunternehmen namens Standard Oil wurde gegründet, Herr Gillette brachte den Einwegrasierer auf den Markt, es gab die Batterie als neue Energiequelle, erfunden von Thomas Edison, und ein neuer Automobilhersteller namens Henry Ford tauchte auf. In diesem Jahrzehnt fanden die erste US-Meisterschaft im Baseball sowie die erste Tour de France statt, und der erste Nobelpreis wurde verliehen. Es war das Zeitalter des Jugendstils, der Brownie-Kamera von Kodak und der Meuterei auf der *Potemkin*. In San Francisco gab es das große Erdbeben, es gab die „Pawlow'schen Hunde" und die „Gibson Girls" von Charles Dana Gibson.

Die Gebrüder Wright flogen eine Maschine, die schwerer als Luft war, über die Sanddünen von Kitty Hawk in North Carolina, und Louis Blériot steuerte das erste Flugzeug über den Ärmelkanal. Es hieß, dass Großbritannien keine Insel mehr war. Spielte das eine Rolle? Es gab ein neues Bündnis zwischen Frankreich und Großbritannien – die Entente cordiale –, ein Versprechen der gegenseitigen Unterstützung und Freundschaft zwischen zwei einstigen Gegnern. Bessere Kommunikationsmöglichkeiten ließen auf ein besseres gegenseitiges Verständnis der Nationen hoffen. Das folgende Jahrzehnt bewies jedoch, dass alte Feindseligkeiten sehr tief saßen …

Introduction

La dernière ligne droite vers la fin du XIXᵉ siècle donna naissance à une myriade d'inventions et d'innovations sous l'impulsion desquelles le nouveau siècle allait prendre son élan. Il y eut le téléphone, le télégraphe, l'automobile, le cinématographe, les rayons X, la découverte de la radioactivité, le gramophone, les fibres synthétiques, le rayon cathodique, la turbine à vapeur et mille autres prodiges, tous nés dans les années 1890. Le vocabulaire de la vie quotidienne et la qualité de la vie se modifièrent pratiquement du tout au tout.

L'un des thèmes majeurs de cette époque était la concurrence : commerciale, militaire, technique ou scientifique. Les grandes puissances européennes étaient les plus concernées et leur concurrence couvrait le globe tout entier. La France, l'Allemagne et la Grande-Bretagne mesuraient leurs capacités industrielles respectives et consacraient de larges ressources à rattraper un éventuel retard ou à maintenir leur prédominance. La Russie impériale suivait tout cela avec inquiétude, tout en contrôlant difficilement sa propre population. Les États-Unis ne demandaient qu'à être laissés en paix et saisissaient la moindre occasion de resserrer leur emprise sur l'Amérique centrale.

Mais à l'écart du laboratoire ou du terrain de parade, loin du chantier naval ou du poste d'usine, toute une agitation frivole continuait. Des foules se rendaient au music-hall, au cabaret, au vaudeville, sur les pistes de danse, au cinéma ou au café. Un verre de vin ou de bière et un mauvais cigare permettaient à chacun de se sentir un Rockefeller. Les femmes, qui commençaient à fumer et à boire en public, se mirent aussi au sport, à tous les sports. Elles apprirent à conduire et à contrôler leur fécondité – mais il était plus facile d'accéder à la conduite qu'à la contraception.

Les riches couraient d'un événement sensationnel à l'autre – l'opéra, les courses, les régates, les bals, les concours de tir, les chasses au renard, les présentations à la cour – car la monarchie avait encore ses partisans. Quant aux pauvres, ils allaient de leur taudis à leur atelier clandestin, même si leurs syndicats gagnaient peu à peu la bataille des salaires, de la réduction du temps de travail et de la sécurité au travail. Un peu partout dans le monde, les suffragettes luttaient pour que les femmes aient le droit de vote. Dans certains pays, elles obtinrent gain de cause. Aux États-Unis, Ellis Island continuait à voir débarquer des foules d'immigrants en quête d'une vie nouvelle, de liberté, d'espoir. Il arrivait que ces rêves se réalisent.

C'est ainsi que débuta le nouveau siècle. À New York et à Paris, on ouvrit le métro. Il y avait une nouvelle compagnie pétrolière, la Standard Oil ; et aussi un nouveau rasoir jetable, lancé sur le marché par un M. Gillette ; une nouvelle source d'énergie appelée « batterie », inventée par Thomas Edison ; une nouvelle société de construction d'automobiles appartenant à Henry Ford. Ce fut la décade des premières Séries mondiales (baseball), du premier Tour de France et aussi des premiers prix Nobel ; celle de l'Art nouveau et de la caméra Brownie ; celle de la mutinerie du *Potemkine* et celle du grand tremblement de terre de San Francisco ; celle des chiens de Pavlov et celle des « girls » de Charles Dana Gibson.

Les frères Wright survolaient les sables de Kitty Hawk, en Caroline-du-Nord, avec un appareil plus lourd que l'air, et Louis Blériot traversait pour la première fois la Manche en aéroplane. La Grande-Bretagne, disait-on, n'était plus une île. Mais quelle importance cela avait-il ? Une nouvelle alliance avait vu le jour entre la France et la Grande-Bretagne, l'Entente cordiale, un pacte d'entraide et d'amitié entre les deux ennemis de toujours. Les nouveaux moyens de communication faisaient croire en une meilleure compréhension entre les peuples. Mais la décade suivante allait montrer que les vieilles rancunes étaient encore profondément enracinées…

1. Cabbages and kings
Herrscher und Beherrschte
Splendeur et misère

The Old Lady of Windsor is finally laid to rest. Crowds line the route of Queen Victoria's funeral cortège as it passes through London in the winter of 1901. For Britain an era had ended, and the 20th century was truly about to begin.

Die Old Lady of Windsor wurde schließlich zur letzten Ruhe gebettet. Eine Menschenmenge säumt den Weg des letzten Geleits von Königin Victoria durch London im Winter 1901. Für Großbritannien war eine Ära zu Ende gegangen und das 20. Jahrhundert fing gerade an, wirklich zu beginnen.

La vieille Lady de Windsor est emportée vers sa dernière demeure. Cet hiver 1901, des foules bordent la route empruntée par le cortège funéraire qui suit à travers Londres l'ultime trajet de la reine Victoria. Pour la Grande-Bretagne, c'est la fin d'une ère et le XXe siècle peut vraiment commencer.

1. Cabbages and kings
Herrscher und Beherrschte
Splendeur et misère

It was the final fling for unashamed splendour – a time when monarchs dressed themselves in all their Ruritanian glory, though it did little for their personal protection. For all their pomp and majesty, few kings slept easily at night.

The extravagantly rich dwelt in marble halls on which they frittered away only a few of the millions that they had made from railways, banking, iron and steel, oil and shipping. The unfortunate masses on the whole respected the lucky few, though organised labour fought more vociferously for better working conditions and shorter hours.

There were signs of change. Democracy was on the advance; socialism was on the march. Norway and Bulgaria gained their independence, while Bosnia and Herzegovina fell under the control of Austria – a change that was to bring misery to millions a decade later. For the first time, the right of the white man to do whatever he wanted was challenged in India and Africa.

Visually, it was a beautiful age. Socially, it was disgraceful. Politically, it was exciting and alarming. But there were always the charms of the Palm Court and the Winter Gardens, and life – for some – was sweeter than it had ever been.

In dieser Zeit stellten die Herrscher ein letztes Mal ganz schamlos ihren Prunk und Glanz zur Schau. Sie kleideten sich prachtvoll, doch half dies wenig, wenn es um ihren persönlichen Schutz ging. Trotz des Prunks und ihrer Erhabenheit konnten nur wenige Könige nachts ruhig schlafen.

Die verschwendungssüchtigen Reichen waren in marmornen Sälen zu Hause. Dafür verprassten sie nur ein paar von den Millionen, die sie durch den Bau von Eisenbahnen, bei der Gründung von Bankhäusern, in der Eisen- und Stahlindustrie, durch die Förderung von Erdöl und durch die Schifffahrt eingenommen hatten. Die breite Masse der Unglücklichen respektierte die wenigen Glücklichen. Dennoch ging die organisierte Arbeiterschaft lautstark für bessere Arbeitsbedingungen und kürzere Arbeitszeiten auf die Straße.

Ein Umbruch stand bevor. Die Demokratie war im Kommen, der Sozialismus auf dem Vormarsch. Norwegen und Bulgarien erlangten ihre Unabhängigkeit, während Bosnien und Herzegowina unter österreichische Herrschaft fielen. Ein Jahrzehnt später sollten diese Veränderungen Millionen von Menschen ins Elend stürzen. Zum ersten Mal wurde das Recht des Weißen, zu tun und zu lassen, was er wollte, in Indien und Afrika angefochten.

Dem Anschein nach war es ein schönes Zeitalter, in sozialer Hinsicht war es jedoch eine Schande. Die Politik war aufregend und spannend, zugleich aber auch beunruhigend und beängstigend. Doch gab es immer den Reiz und Charme der mit Palmen ausgestatteten stattlichen Wohnhäuser und der Wintergärten. Das Leben war – jedenfalls für einige Menschen – leichtlebiger und angenehmer als jemals zuvor.

Les cours royales jetaient les derniers feux d'une splendeur éhontée : les monarques se paraient des atours d'une gloire immense mais ces apparats protégeaient mal leurs personnes des dangers. Le faste et la majesté assuraient à peu de rois des nuits paisibles.

Les riches à outrance dilapidaient avec peine quelques-uns des millions que leur rapportaient les chemins de fer, la banque, le fer et l'acier, le pétrole et l'export. Les moins fortunés respectaient le petit nombre de ces chanceux, mais les syndicats luttaient de plus en plus âprement pour de meilleures conditions de travail et des journées plus courtes.

Il y avait des signes de changement. La démocratie avançait ; le socialisme était en marche. La Norvège et la Bulgarie obtinrent leur indépendance tandis que la Bosnie-Herzégovine tombait sous contrôle autrichien – un événement qui allait apporter la misère à des millions de personnes une décennie plus tard. Pour la première fois, le bon plaisir de l'homme blanc se heurtait à une puissante résistance en Inde et en Afrique.

Ce fut une belle époque mais qui fut aussi marquée par l'indignité sociale. Politiquement, elle fut riche de promesses comme de menaces. Mais, il y avait toujours les charmes des palmeraies intérieures et la vie, pour certains, n'avait jamais été aussi douce.

On to centre stage steps a new monarch:
Edward VII poses for his likeness, c. 1901.
He was 60 years old when he succeeded
to the throne.

Ein neuer König betritt die Szene:
Edward VII. steht Modell für ein Porträt,
um 1901. Er war 60 Jahre alt, als er die
Thronfolge antrat.

Un nouveau monarque s'avance sur le devant
de la scène : Édouard VII pose pour son
portrait, vers 1901. Il avait 60 ans lorsqu'il
monta sur le trône d'Angleterre.

A less than flattering
view of the new King
of England, taken
at Sandringham,
the royal estate in
Norfolk, c. 1901.

Eine wenig schmei-
chelhafte Ansicht des
neuen Königs von
England, aufgenom-
men in Sandringham,
dem königlichen Sitz
in Norfolk, um 1901.

Une vision peu
flatteuse du nouveau
roi d'Angleterre à
Sandringham, la
résidence royale dans
le Norfolk, vers 1901.

Reinhold Thiele's portrait of Stephanus Johannes Paulus Kruger, leader of the Boers in their fight against Britain. After early successes, the Boers were now heading for defeat.

Reinhold Thieles Porträt von Stephanus Johannes Paulus Kruger, Anführer der Buren im Kampf gegen Großbritannien. Nach anfänglichen Erfolgen steuerten die Buren nun auf eine Niederlage zu.

Portrait, par Reinhold Thiele, de Stephanus Johannes Paulus Kruger, chef des Boers en lutte contre la Grande-Bretagne. Après plusieurs succès, les Boers s'acheminaient vers la défaite.

The last Tsar. (Opposite) Kaiser Wilhelm II of Germany extends
his hand to his cousin, Tsar Nicholas II of Russia. (Above) Nicholas
consults his liver specialist before taking a trip on the royal yacht.

Der letzte Zar. (Gegenüberliegende Seite) Der deutsche Kaiser
Wilhelm II. reicht seinem Cousin, dem russischen Zaren Nikolaus II.,
die Hand. (Oben) Vor einer Fahrt auf der königlichen Yacht konsultiert
Nikolaus II. seinen Leberspezialisten.

Le dernier tsar. (Ci-contre) L'empereur allemand Guillaume II tend la
main à son cousin, le tsar Nicolas II de Russie. (Ci-dessus) Nicolas II
consulte son spécialiste du foie, avant d'entamer un voyage sur le
yacht royal.

An upset during a picnic
attended by the Russian royal
family, c. 1909. There were far
worse upsets ahead for Nicholas
and his daughter.

Eine böse Überraschung
während eines Picknicks mit
der russischen Zarenfamilie,
um 1909. Nikolaus und
seiner Tochter standen noch
weitaus schlimmere Über-
raschungen bevor.

Crise mineure lors d'un pique-
nique réunissant la famille
royale russe, vers 1909. Des
désordres bien plus graves
attendaient Nicolas et sa fille.

Vladimir Ilyich
Lenin bides his time
and makes his plans
for the revolution
that was to tear
Russia and the
world apart, 1901.

Wladimir Iljitsch
Lenin wartet auf den
richtigen Augenblick
und schmiedet Pläne
für die Revolution,
die einen Keil zwi-
schen Russland und
den Rest der Welt
treiben sollte, 1901.

Vladimir Ilitch
Lénine prend son
temps et prépare
déjà la révolution qui
déchirera la Russie et
le monde, 1901.

President William McKinley of the United States addresses a crowd shortly after his re-election in 1900. McKinley's money-making policies were enormously popular.

Der Präsident der Vereinigten Staaten, William McKinley, hält kurz nach seiner Wiederwahl im Jahre 1900 eine Rede vor einer Menschenmenge. Die Gewinn bringende Politik von McKinley war äußerst beliebt.

Le président des États-Unis, William McKinley, s'adresse à la foule peu après sa réélection en 1900. La politique de McKinley remplissait les caisses et remportait l'adhésion…

...but not with everyone. A year later, McKinley was shot by an anarchist named Leon Czolgosz at a rally in Buffalo. He died eight days later. McKinley's funeral took place on a rain-drenched day in Washington, DC.

... aber nicht bei jedermann. Ein Jahr später wurde McKinley von einem Anarchisten namens Leon Czolgosz bei einer Versammlung in Buffalo angeschossen. Er starb acht Tage später. McKinleys Beisetzung fand an einem regnerischen Tag in Washington, D.C., statt.

... mais pas de tous. Un an plus tard, un anarchiste du nom de Leon Czolgosz tirait sur McKinley qui mourut huit jours plus tard. Les funérailles eurent lieu sous la pluie à Washington D.C.

On the streets…Winston Spencer Churchill, President of the
Board of Trade, campaigns on the top of a taxi, seeking support
for his new Liberal policies, Manchester, April 1908.

Auf der Straße … Winston Spencer Churchill, britischer
Handelsminister, wirbt vom Dach eines Taxis aus für Anhänger
seiner neuen liberalen Politik, Manchester, April 1908.

Dans les rues… Winston Spencer Churchill, ministre du
Commerce, fait campagne du haut du toit d'un taxi, cherchant
des soutiens pour sa nouvelle politique libérale, à Manchester,
en avril 1908.

On the stump… Theodore Roosevelt, Governor of New York State, addresses a crowd of suffragettes from the verandah of his home, 1900. 'Votes for Women' was never high on his political agenda.

Auf der Rednertribüne … Theodore Roosevelt, Gouverneur des Staates New York, hält von der Veranda seines Hauses aus eine Rede vor einer Menge von Frauenrechtlerinnen, 1900. „Wahlrecht für Frauen" stand nie an oberster Stelle seines politischen Programms.

De sa véranda… Theodore Roosevelt, gouverneur de l'État de New York, s'adresse à une foule de suffragettes, en 1900. Le vote des femmes ne fut jamais au premier rang de ses priorités.

The white man's game. A young Mohandas Gandhi poses outside his law office in Natal, c. 1903. He had given up a £5,000 a year law practice in Bombay.

Der Zeitvertreib des weißen Mannes. Der junge Mahatma Gandhi posiert vor seiner Anwaltskanzlei in Natal, um 1903. In Bombay hatte er seine Kanzlei, die ihm jährlich £ 5000 einbrachte, aufgegeben.

Le jeu de l'homme blanc. Le jeune Mohandas Gandhi pose devant son cabinet d'avocat, Natal, vers 1903. Peu auparavant, il s'était retiré de son cabinet de Bombay qui lui rapportait 5000 livres par an.

The Welshman's game. David Lloyd George and his faithful pug ponder the future, c. 1904. Within the next few years, Lloyd George would do much to challenge the power of inherited wealth.

Der Zeitvertreib des walisischen Mannes. David Lloyd George und sein treuer Mops machen sich Gedanken über die Zukunft, um 1904. In den folgenden Jahren setzte sich Lloyd George sehr dafür ein, die Macht des durch Erbe erlangten Reichtums in Frage zu stellen.

Le jeu du Gallois. David Lloyd George et son fidèle carlin considèrent l'avenir, vers 1904. Au cours des années suivantes, Lloyd George fera beaucoup pour limiter la puissance des grandes fortunes.

Jean Jaurès (third from the left) chats with colleagues on
a French street, c. 1901. Jaurès was the founder of both
the French Socialist Party and the left-wing newspaper
L'Humanité.

Jean Jaurès (Dritter von links) plaudert mit Kollegen auf
einer Straße in Frankreich, um 1901. Jaurès war Gründer der
französischen sozialistischen Partei und der linksgerichteten
Zeitung *L'Humanité*.

Jean Jaurès (le troisième à partir de la gauche) discute avec des
collègues tout en marchant, vers 1901. Il fut le fondateur du
Parti socialiste français et du journal de gauche *L'Humanité*.

Ramsay MacDonald – significantly, the only man not wearing a hat, as fashion then decreed – at a Labour Party demonstration in 1909. MacDonald was one of the founders of the British Labour Party.

Ramsay MacDonald – auffällig ist, dass er als Einziger keinen Hut trägt, der damals groß in Mode war – auf einer Versammlung der Labour Party im Jahre 1909. MacDonald war einer der Gründer der britischen Labour Party.

Ramsay MacDonald – qui, de manière significative, ne porte pas de chapeau, cette mode étant alors décriée – lors d'une manifestation du Parti travailliste britannique, en 1909. MacDonald avait été l'un des fondateurs de ce parti.

Immigrant millionaire. Andrew Carnegie, the Scottish industrialist and philanthropist, at his desk, c. 1900. Carnegie made his fortune in the United States' iron and steel industries.

Ein immigrierter Millionär. Andrew Carnegie, der schottische Industrielle und Menschenfreund, an seinem Schreibtisch, um 1900. Carnegie machte sein Geld in der Eisen- und Stahlindustrie der Vereinigten Staaten.

Un millionnaire immigré. Andrew Carnegie, industriel et philantrope écossais, à son bureau, vers 1900. Carnegie avait fait fortune aux États-Unis, dans l'industrie du fer et de l'acier.

Home-bred millionaire. John Pierpoint Morgan, the American financier, banker and art collector, c. 1909. Morgan founded the US Steel Corporation.

Ein einheimischer Millionär. John Pierpoint Morgan, amerikanischer Finanzier, Bankier und Kunstsammler, um 1909. Morgan gründete die US Steel Corporation.

Un millionnaire du cru. John Pierpoint Morgan, financier, banquier et collectionneur d'art américain, vers 1909. Morgan avait fondé la US Steel Corporation.

2. Conflict
Konflikte
Les conflits

The British Naval Brigade shell Boer positions during the Battle of Magersfontein in the Second Boer War, December 1900. The gun was known as 'Joe Chamberlain' after the Secretary for the Colonies. Hauling it over the rough terrain was a formidable achievement, later celebrated in the annual field-gun competition at the Royal Tournament.

Die britische Seeflotte nimmt Burenposten im Kampf von Magersfontein im Zweiten Burenkrieg unter Beschuss, Dezember 1900. Das Geschütz war nach dem Minister für die Kolonien, „Joe Chamberlain", benannt. Eine Meisterleistung, da man dieses Geschütz über das holprige Gelände ziehen konnte. Später wurde es im jährlichen Feldgeschütz-Wettkampf beim Royal Tournament groß gefeiert.

La brigade navale britannique bombardant des positions boers pendant la bataille de Magersfontein lors de la deuxième guerre des Boers, en décembre 1900. Le canon s'appelait « Joe Chamberlain », du nom du Secrétaire des colonies. Le seul fait d'avoir réussi à le tracter sur un terrain aussi accidenté était une formidable performance qui fut plus tard saluée au concours annuel de canon du Tournoi royal.

2. Conflict
Konflikte
Les conflits

War was a splendid thing. There were fine new toys to play with – bigger guns than ever before, torpedoes, great battleships, submarines, and even early chemical weapons. Few thought that the fledgling aeroplane would be of any use, but there was still the cavalry to add tone to what would otherwise have been a mere vulgar brawl.

And there were plenty of places in which these new weapons could be tried out. The British army was active in South Africa from 1899 to 1902, in Tibet in 1903 and in India throughout the entire decade. Germany and France kept a watchful and suspicious eye on the annual manoeuvres of each other's armies and navies. Russia marched proudly into Manchuria in 1900 and suffered an ignominious defeat at the hands of the Japanese in 1905.

Civil disturbances abounded. There were riots in Madrid in 1900, and a near-revolution in Barcelona nine years later. The Boxer Rebellion against foreign interference in Chinese affairs was crushed with savage cruelty.

And, though few realised it at the time, when the Young Bosnia movement began terrorist activities against the Austro-Hungarian Empire, the time to open the boxes of the new toys of destruction came considerably nearer.

Krieg war eine großartige Angelegenheit. Es gab ausgezeichnete neue „Spielzeuge" – größere Kanonen denn je, Torpedos, große Schlachtschiffe, U-Boote und sogar erste chemische Waffen. Nur wenige Menschen glaubten daran, dass das gerade erfundene Flugzeug von irgendeinem Nutzen sein würde. Doch die Kavallerie konnte ja immer noch dem etwas mehr Niveau verleihen, was sonst nur eine wilde Rauferei gewesen wäre.

Es gab reichlich Plätze, an denen diese neuen Waffen ausprobiert werden konnten. Von 1899 bis 1902 kämpfte die britische Armee in Südafrika, 1903 in Tibet und während dieser gesamten Zeitspanne in Indien. Deutschland und Frankreich wachten mit Argusaugen über die jährlichen Gefechtsübungen der Armeen und Kriegsflotten des anderen. Im Jahre 1900 fiel Russland siegessicher in der Mandschurei ein, erlitt dann jedoch eine bittere Niederlage durch die Japaner im Jahre 1905.

Bürgerunruhen waren an der Tagesordnung. 1900 kam es zu Ausschreitungen in Madrid und neun Jahre später beinahe zu einer Revolution in Barcelona. Dem Boxeraufstand gegen die Einmischung des Auslands in China wurde mit Gewalt ein Ende gesetzt.

Als die junge bosnische Bewegung mit terroristischen Anschlägen gegen das österreich-ungarische Kaiserreich vorging, rückte die Zeit, die neuen „Vernichtungsspielzeuge" hervorzuholen, immer näher, obwohl dies nur wenigen bewusst war.

Dieu que la guerre était belle! On disposait de tout un arsenal de nouveaux jouets: des canons plus énormes que jamais, des torpilles, de formidables navires de guerre, des sous-marins et même les premières armes chimiques. Peu croyaient à l'utilité des nouveaux aéroplanes, mais la cavalerie était encore là pour donner un peu d'allure à ce qui n'eût été autrement qu'une vulgaire rixe.

Et les occasions ne manquaient pas d'essayer ces nouvelles armes. L'armée britannique s'engagea en Afrique du Sud de 1899 à 1902, au Tibet en 1903 et en Inde constamment. L'Allemagne et la France considéraient d'un regard soupçonneux et attentif les manœuvres de leurs armées et de leurs marines réciproques. La Russie marcha fièrement sur la Mandchourie en 1900 et subit une humiliante défaite devant les Japonais en 1905.

Les désordres civils se multipliaient. Il y eut des émeutes à Madrid en 1900 et presque une révolution à Barcelone, neuf ans plus tard. La Révolte des Boxers, contre l'interférence étrangère dans les affaires chinoises, fut écrasée avec une brutale cruauté.

Et même si peu d'observateurs en étaient vraiment conscients à l'époque, lorsque le jeune mouvement bosniaque commença à se livrer à des activités terroristes contre l'Empire austro-hongrois, l'heure était proche où les nouveaux jouets de destruction allaient enfin pouvoir servir.

A group of British prisoners of war in the early days of the Boer War (1899–1902). On the right is Winston Churchill, twenty-five-year-old war correspondent of the *Morning Post*. He escaped and hurried back to England, where he became an MP.

Eine Gruppe von britischen Kriegsgefangenen zu Beginn des Burenkrieges (1899–1902). Rechts außen Winston Churchill, damals 25 Jahre alt und Kriegsberichterstatter für die *Morning Post*. Er konnte fliehen und kehrte schnell nach England zurück, wo er Abgeordneter im britischen Unterhaus wurde.

Un groupe de prisonniers de guerre britanniques aux premiers jours de la guerre des Boers (1899–1902). À droite, Winston Churchill, 25 ans, correspondant du *Morning Post*. Il réussit à s'évader et à regagner l'Angleterre, où il devint député.

Armed Afrikaaners (Boers) pose for the camera during the siege of Ladysmith, 1900. The Boers were well-armed, superbly mounted and experts in *veldt* craft, but their early victories gave way to a series of bitter defeats.

Bewaffnete Afrikaaner (Buren) posieren während der Belagerung von Ladysmith, 1900, für die Kamera. Die Buren waren gut mit Waffen ausgerüstet, hatten ausgezeichnete Pferde und waren Experten darin, sich in der afrikanischen Buschlandschaft zurechtzufinden. Doch ihre frühen Siege wurden von einer Reihe bitterer Niederlagen abgelöst.

Des Afrikaners armés, les Boers, posant pour la photo au cours du siège de Ladysmith, en 1900. Les Boers étaient bien armés, excellents cavaliers et connaissaient le veldt (steppe de l'Afrique du Sud) à la perfection. Malgré cela, leurs premières victoires firent bientôt place à une série d'amères défaites.

British dead in front of a Boer defence post. Losses on both sides were heavy during the Boer War. The British were unused to a war of movement, and to the guerrilla tactics of the Boers. They were also incompetently led.

Britische Gefallene vor einem Verteidigungsposten der Buren. Auf beiden Seiten gab es beträchtliche Verluste während des Burenkrieges. Die Briten waren einen Bewegungskampf und die Guerilla-Taktiken der Buren nicht gewohnt. Darüber hinaus war ihre Führung nicht kompetent.

Des morts britanniques devant un poste de défense des Boers. Des deux côtés, les pertes occasionnées furent très lourdes. Les Britanniques n'avaient pas la pratique des guerres de mouvement et des tactiques de guérilla des Boers. De plus, leur direction militaire était incompétente.

Reinhold Thiele's study of Boer dead on the battlefield of Spion Kop, 24 January 1900. It had been typical battle of the war, a desperate struggle for possession of high ground that was ultimately of little use to either side.

Reinhold Thieles Aufnahme von Gefallenen auf der Seite der Buren auf dem Schlachtfeld von Spion Kop, 24. Januar 1900. Eine typische kriegerische Auseinandersetzung und ein verzweifelter Kampf um den Besitz von fruchtbarem Boden, der letzten Endes für beide Seiten kaum von Nutzen war.

Une étude de Reinhold Thiele : des morts boers sur le champ de bataille de Spion Kop, le 24 janvier 1900. Ce fut l'une des batailles caractéristiques de cette guerre, une lutte désespérée pour le contrôle d'un plateau qui devait s'avérer en fin de compte de peu d'utilité.

Another of Reinhold Thiele's grimly beautiful images from the Boer War. A blindfolded German intermediary is brought in from the Boer lines to negotiate a surrender, 17 March 1900.

Eine weitere faszinierende, wenn auch trostlose Aufnahme Reinhold Thieles aus dem Burenkrieg. Mit verbundenen Augen wird ein deutscher Mittelsmann von Burenposten weggeführt, um über eine Kapitulation zu verhandeln, 17. März 1900.

Une autre de ces images de Reinhold Thiele, sombrement belle, prise pendant la guerre des Boers. Un médiateur allemand, les yeux bandés, est amené des lignes boers pour négocier une capitulation, le 17 mars 1900.

Warriors all. British infantry, wearing pith helmets and the new khaki
uniforms, charge a *kopje* with bayonets fixed, c. 1900. Although often posed
especially for the camera, such pictures were good for morale at home.

Krieger gegen Krieger. Britische Infanteristen mit Tropenhelmen und neuen
Khakiuniformen erstürmen mit Gewehren eine kleine Hügelkuppe (kopje),
um 1900. Wenn solche Bilder auch oftmals extra für die Kamera gestellt
waren, so stärkten sie doch die Moral in der Heimat.

Tous des guerriers. L'infanterie britannique, portant casques coloniaux et
nouveaux uniformes kaki, chargeant une petite colline isolée, baïonnettes
aux poings. Ces photos étaient généralement mises en scène et servaient à
entretenir le moral de ceux qui étaient restés en Grande-Bretagne.

The backbone of Boer resistance – Afrikaaners in their farming clothes, armed with bolt action rifles, c. 1900.

Das Rückgrat des Burenwiderstandes – Afrikaaner in ihrer Bauernkluft mit Gewehren, um 1900.

Le pivot de la résistance des Boers – des Afrikaners dans leurs habits de paysans, armés de fusils à culasses, vers 1900.

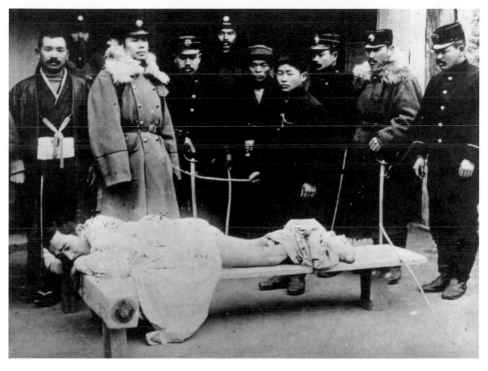

Neither photographers nor their clients were squeamish in the early 20th century.
(Opposite) The public execution of one of the leaders of the Boxer Rebellion in China, 1900.
(Above) Japanese troops beat a Korean prisoner to force a confession from him, 1905.

Anfang des 20. Jahrhunderts waren weder Fotografen noch ihre Modelle zimperlich.
(Gegenüberliegende Seite) Die öffentliche Hinrichtung eines Anführers des Boxeraufstandes
in China, 1900. (Oben) Japanische Truppenangehörige schlagen einen koreanischen
Gefangenen, um ihn zu einem Geständnis zu zwingen, 1905.

Pas plus les photographes que leurs clients n'étaient facilement effarouchés, au début du XXe
siècle. (Ci-contre) L'exécution publique de l'un des chefs de la Révolte des Boxers, en Chine,
en 1900. (Ci-dessus) Des soldats japonais fouettent un prisonnier coréen pour en obtenir des
aveux, en 1905.

The streets of
Yokohama are
decorated to
celebrate a Japanese
victory in the war
with Russia, 1905.

Zur Feier eines
Sieges der Japaner
im Krieg gegen
Russland sind
die Straßen in
Yokohama reich
geschmückt, 1905.

Les rues de Yoko-
hama décorées en
l'honneur d'une
victoire japonaise,
dans la guerre contre
la Russie, 1905.

After the Battle of Port Arthur, the Russian battleship *Tsarevich* limps into Kinchan harbour, 10 August 1904. The surprise defeat of mighty Russia was greeted with approval by most Western countries.

Nach der Schlacht von Port Arthur kommt das russische Schlachtschiff *Zarewitsch* mit Müh und Not im Hafen von Kinchan an, 10. August 1904. Die überraschende Niederlage des mächtigen Russland wurde von den meisten westlichen Ländern mit großer Zustimmung begrüßt.

Après la bataille de Port Arthur, le 10 août 1904, le cuirassé russe *Tsarevitch* entre tant bien que mal dans le port de Kinchan. La surprenante défaite de la puissante Russie fut accueillie favorablement par la plupart des pays occidentaux.

The Russian rising
of 1905 was brutally
repressed by the
Tsar's troops and
police. The coffins
of some of those
killed are carried
through the streets.

Der Arbeiterauf-
stand in Russland
von 1905 wurde
von den Truppen
des Zaren und
der Polizei blutig
niedergeschlagen.
Die Särge einiger
der Getöteten
werden durch die
Straßen getragen.

La révolution russe
de 1905 fut brutale-
ment réprimée
par l'armée et la
police du tsar. Ici,
l'on porte dans les
rues les dépouilles
de ceux qui furent
ainsi tués.

The *Potemkin*
mutiny, June 1905.
In the white shirt
is Matuchenko,
one of the leaders
of the uprising.

Die Meuterei
auf dem Panzer-
kreuzer *Potemkin*,
Juni 1905. Vorne
im weißen Hemd
steht Matuchenko,
einer der Anführer
des Aufstandes.

La mutinerie du
Potemkine, juin
1905. L'homme
en blanc est
Matuchenko,
l'un des chefs
du soulèvement.

After their failure to inspire a mutiny throughout the Russian fleet, members of the crew of the battleship *Potemkin* sought political asylum in the Romanian port of Constanta, 22 July 1905. They were favourably received.

Nachdem es nicht gelungen war, eine Meuterei auf der gesamten russischen Schwarzmeerflotte zu entfachen, suchten Besatzungsmitglieder des Kriegs schiffes *Potemkin* politisches Asyl im rumänischen Hafen von Konstanza, 22. Juli 1905. Dort wurden sie mit offenen Armen empfangen.

Après leur échec à entraîner dans la mutinerie l'ensemble de la flotte russe, des membres de l'équipage du cuirassé *Potemkine* cherchèrent un asile politique, le 22 juillet 1905, dans le port roumain de Constanta, où ils furent bien accueillis.

Official massacre. Bodies of Russian Jews killed during the rising of 1905
await burial in a cemetery. The suppression of the rising was used as an
excuse to revile, persecute and slaughter many Jews.

Angeordnetes Massaker. Leichen russischer Juden, die während des Aufstandes von 1905 umgebracht wurden, warten auf ihr Begräbnis auf einem
Friedhof. Die Unterdrückung des Aufstandes benutzte man als Vorwand
dafür, viele Juden zu diskriminieren, zu verfolgen und zu ermorden.

Massacres officiels. Les corps de juifs russes tués au cours de la Révolution
de 1905 attendent d'être inhumés dans un cimetière. La répression du
soulèvement servit de prétexte pour vilipender, persécuter et massacrer de
nombreux juifs.

Mob rule. The body
of Louis Higgins
hangs from a bridge
in Texas after he had
been lynched in the
summer of 1907.

Herrschaft des
Pöbels. Die Leiche
von Louis Higgins
baumelt an einer
Brücke in Texas,
nachdem er im Som-
mer 1907 ermordet
worden war.

La loi du nombre.
Le corps de Louis
Higgins, accroché
à un pont dans le
Texas, après avoir
été lynché, au cours
de l'été 1907.

Women arrive to cast their votes for the first time in Wellington North, 1909.
Although New Zealand became the first country to allow women the right
to vote, sadly at the time events there had little effect on the rest of the world.

Zum ersten Mal geben Frauen ihre Stimme in Wellington North ab, 1909.
Obwohl Neuseeland als erstes Land Frauen das Wahlrecht einräumte, hatten
die dortigen Ereignisse damals bedauerlicherweise nur wenig Auswirkung auf
den Rest der Welt.

Des femmes viennent voter pour la première fois à Wellington North, en 1909.
La Nouvelle-Zélande fut le premier pays à accorder le droit de vote aux
femmes, mais à cette époque un tel événement trouva peu d'écho dans le reste
du monde.

In Britain the battle had not yet been won. Lady Emmeline Pethick-Lawrence, one of the leaders of the suffragette movement, addresses a crowd in Trafalgar Square, London, 1908. She received a mixed reception.

In Großbritannien hatte man den Kampf noch nicht gewonnen. Lady Emmeline Pethick-Lawrence, eine der Anführerinnen der Frauenrechtsbewegung, hält eine Rede am Trafalgar Square, London, 1908. Diese wurde mit gemischten Gefühlen aufgenommen.

En Grande-Bretagne, la bataille n'était pas encore gagnée. Lady Emmeline Pethick-Lawrence, l'une des dirigeantes du mouvement des suffragettes, s'adresse à la foule à Trafalgar Square, Londres, 1908. L'accueil fut mitigé.

Emmeline Pankhurst
(left) and her daugh-
ter Christabel,
founders of the
Women's Social
and Political Union,
in prison clothes,
21 October 1908.

Emmeline Pankhurst
(links) und ihre
Tochter Christabel in
Gefängniskleidung,
21. Oktober 1908.
Sie gründeten die
Women's Social
and Political Union
(WSPU).

21 octobre 1908.
Emmeline Pankhurst
(à gauche) et sa
fille Christabel,
fondatrices de
l'Union sociale
et politique des
femmes (Women's
Social and Political
Union), en habits
de prisonnières.

Anti-suffragette
propaganda. The
beautiful (and there-
fore apolitical) Mary
Pickford laughingly
reads a suffragette
news sheet of 1909.

Anti-Suffragetten-
propaganda. Die
schöne, aber unpoli-
tische Mary Pickford
liest belustigt
ein Zeitungsblatt
der Frauenrechts-
bewegung aus dem
Jahre 1909.

Propagande anti-
suffragettes. La belle
(et, bien entendu,
apolitique) Mary
Pickford lit en
riant un journal
revendiquant le
droit de vote pour
les femmes.

French police assault a striking worker as he leaves a meeting in the St Paul district of Paris, c. 1909. There was considerable industrial unrest throughout Europe at this time, and similar police harassment in most countries.

Die französische Polizei greift einen streikenden Arbeiter an, als dieser eine Versammlung im Pariser Stadtteil St. Paul verlässt, um 1909. Zu dieser Zeit waren bei Arbeiterunruhen Schikanen von Seiten der Polizei in vielen europäischen Ländern an der Tagesordnung.

La police française assaillant un ouvrier en grève au moment où il quitte une réunion dans le quartier Saint-Paul à Paris, vers 1909. À l'époque, l'agitation sociale était considérable dans toute l'Europe et un harcèlement policier comparable existait dans la plupart des pays.

A group of unemployed demonstrate for the right to work, London, 1 October 1908. The banner reads 'Work or Riot – One or the Other'. It was a bold and criminal slogan, which could have earned all of them a spell in gaol.

Eine Gruppe von Arbeitslosen demonstriert für das Recht auf Arbeit, London, 1. Oktober 1908. Auf dem Transparent prangt das Motto: „Entweder Arbeit oder Aufstand." Ein mutiger, aber auch strafbarer Slogan, für den jeder der Demonstranten für eine Weile hinter Gitter hätte wandern können.

Un groupe d'ouvriers au chômage manifeste pour le droit au travail, à Londres, 1ᵉʳ octobre 1908. La bannière porte le slogan «Travail ou émeutes – c'est l'un ou l'autre!». Ce slogan provocant et hors-la-loi faisait encourir la prison à tous les manifestants.

3. Peoples
Völker
Peuples

Spencer Arnold's photograph of a young Sinhalese girl in 1900.
By then, the camera had done much to familiarise Westerners with
their fellow human beings from all over the world, though many
still viewed them as curiosities.

Aufnahme von einem jungen singhalesischen Mädchen im Jahre 1900
von Spencer Arnold. Zu der Zeit hatte die Kamera den Menschen im
Westen bereits große Dienste im Hinblick darauf geleistet, sich mit
ihren Mitmenschen auf der ganzen Welt vertraut zu machen. Jedoch
empfanden viele sie immer noch als sehr fremd.

Photographie de Spencer Arnold : une jeune fille cinghalaise en 1900.
À cette époque, la photo avait beaucoup fait pour familiariser les
Occidentaux avec leurs congénères du monde entier. Malgré cela,
beaucoup étaient encore considérés comme des curiosités.

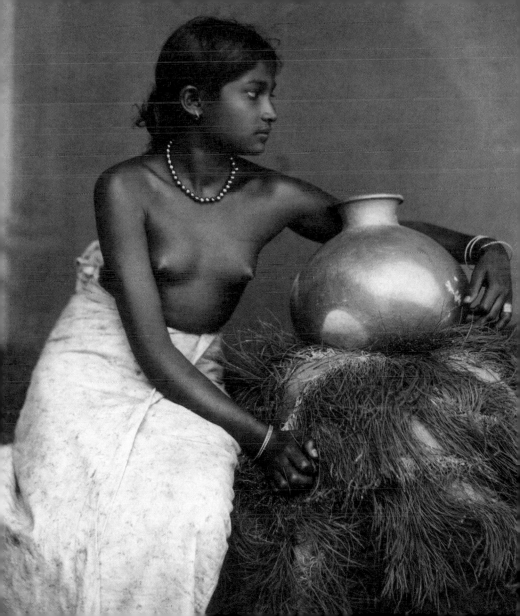

3. Peoples
Völker
Peuples

For a while it seemed possible that the inhabitants of the world might lose their fear of each other. The railway and the steamship had brought the exotic within comparatively easy reach, and even the poor became familiar with their opposite numbers from the other side of the globe as immigrant workers poured into Western Europe and the United States. But 'foreigners' were still regarded with suspicion and were looked upon as oddities, freaks and delinquents by many of the Christian West.

At best, Westerners viewed the inhabitants of far-flung continents as quaint, though there were plenty who were moved by portraits of dusky maidens or young African warriors in ways that Dr Sigmund Freud was just beginning to reveal. The notion that people in the northern latitudes were somehow superior to those of the tropics was firmly established in many minds, and 'Hottentots' were unfavourably compared with 'Eskimos'. The former were charming but idle; the latter were plain but industrious.

And yet, forcing its way through this barrier of prejudice and racism was a new breed of scientists. Émile Durkheim's methods of examining societies, pioneered in the early 1900s, were seized upon by anthropologists. The world was coming into sharper focus.

Eine Zeit lang schien es so, als würden die Menschen auf der Welt ihre Furcht voreinander ablegen können. Durch die Eisenbahn und das Dampfschiff war das Fremde in Reichweite gelangt. Sogar die armen Leute lernten ihre Mitmenschen von der anderen Seite des Globus kennen, als ausländische Arbeiter nach Westeuropa und in die Vereinigten Staaten strömten. Man begegnete „Ausländern" jedoch noch mit einem gewissen Misstrauen und diese galten bei vielen im christlichen Westen als Sonderlinge, Spinner und Verbrecher. Der Westen sah die Einwohner entfernter Kontinente als seltsam an, dennoch gab es Viele, die von den

Porträts dunkelhäutiger Mädchen oder junger afrikanischer Krieger bewegt waren, ein Phänomen, das Dr. Sigmund Freud gerade ans Licht brachte. Die Vorstellung, die Menschen in den nördlichen Breiten seien mehr Wert als die der tropischen Regionen, hatte sich in den Köpfen festgesetzt. Man verglich die „Hottentotten" mit den „Eskimos". Die Ersteren waren charmant, aber faul, die Letzteren unscheinbar, aber dafür fleißig.

Und dennoch war es ein neuer wissenschaftlicher Ansatz, diese Barrieren von Vorurteilen und Rassismus zu durchbrechen. Die von Émile Durkheim angewandten Methoden zur Untersuchung von Gesellschaften nahmen Anfang des 20. Jahrhunderts eine Vorreiterrolle ein und wurden mit großem Interesse von den Anthropologen aufgenommen. Die Welt wurde nun in ein klareres Licht gerückt.

Pendant un temps, il sembla possible que les habitants de la planète se débarrassent de leur méfiance réciproque. Le chemin de fer et le bateau à vapeur avaient rapproché les pays exotiques et mêmes les moins riches se familiarisaient avec leurs homologues du bout du monde. Les travailleurs immigrés arrivaient en masse en Europe occidentale et aux États-Unis. Mais les « étrangers » étaient toujours dévisagés d'un regard soupçonneux et considérés comme des curiosités ou des délinquants par de nombreux habitants de l'Occident chrétien.

Au mieux, les Occidentaux trouvaient étranges ces habitants des continents éloignés, même si beaucoup étaient frappés par ces portraits de jeunes filles à la peau sombre ou de guerriers africains, phénomène que le Dr Sigmund Freud analysa à cette époque. L'idée que les peuples du nord étaient, d'une manière ou d'une autre, supérieurs à ceux qui vivaient sous les tropiques était enracinée dans de nombreux esprits et on comparait les « hottentots » aux « esquimaux » à la défaveur des premiers. Ceux-ci étaient jugés charmants mais paresseux, tandis que les seconds, que l'on jugeait moins beaux, étaient plus industrieux.

Et pourtant, forçant le chemin à travers ce mur de préjugés et de racisme, une nouvelle génération de scientifiques apparaissait. La méthode sociologique d'Émile Durkheim, forgée au début des années 1900, fut adoptée par les anthropologues. On commençait à voir le monde d'une manière plus fine.

Few realised at the time that the camera was recording vanishing civilisations. The early 20th century had little respect for other cultures.

Nur Wenigen war bewusst, dass mit der Kamera aussterbende Zivilisationen im Bild festgehalten wurden. Anfang des 20. Jahrhunderts hatte man wenig Respekt vor fremden Kulturen.

On réalisait peu, à l'époque, que l'appareil photo était en train d'enregistrer les dernières traces de civilisations en voie de disparition. Le XXᵉ siècle naissant avait peu de respect pour les autres cultures.

(Opposite) A Maori
man in ceremonial
robes, 1900.
(Right) A Maori
woman on the porch
of an elaborately
decorated house.

(Gegenüberliegende
Seite) Ein Maori-
Mann im rituellen
Gewand, 1900.
(Rechts) Eine Maori-
Frau vor dem Portal
eines kunstvoll
verzierten Hauses.

(Ci-contre) Un
homme maori
en costume de
cérémonie, 1900.
(À droite) Une
femme maorie
sur le porche
d'une maison très
ornementée.

A young girl from
the north-east
Indian state of
Manipur carrying
a large umbrella.

Ein kleines Mädchen
aus Manipur,
einem Bundesstaat
im nordöstlichen
Indien. In der Hand
hält es einen großen
Schirm.

Portant un grand
parapluie, une petite
fille du Manipur,
un État du nord-est
de l'Inde.

A Hindu fakir and other holy men from the city of Benares, on the River Ganges, 1909.
Of all Britain's colonies, India was the most prized, the 'jewel in the crown', a land large
enough to maintain much of its own culture.

Ein hinduistischer Fakir und zwei andere heilige Männer aus der Stadt Benares am Ganges,
1909. Von allen britischen Kolonien war Indien die beliebteste – das so genannte „Kronjuwel".
Das Land war groß genug, um die einheimische Kultur weitgehend bewahren zu können.

Un fakir hindouiste et d'autres saints hommes de la ville de Bénarès, sur le Gange, en 1909.
De toutes les colonies britanniques, l'Inde était la plus prisée, la « perle de la couronne » ;
le pays était aussi assez grand pour maintenir intacte une grande part de sa culture.

Wherever they lived, European Jews preserved their way of life, their culture and their language – though they were often persecuted and driven from their homes in the pogroms of Eastern Europe. Here Polish Jews pose for the camera, c. 1900.

Wo sie auch lebten, bewahrten die europäischen Juden immer ihre Lebensweise, ihre Kultur und ihre Sprache, obwohl sie während der Pogrome in Osteuropa oft verfolgt und aus ihren Häusern gejagt wurden. Hier lassen sich polnische Juden fotografieren, um 1900.

Où qu'ils vivent, les juifs d'Europe avaient réussi à préserver leur manière de vivre, leur culture et leur langue, en dépit des nombreuses persécutions et des pogromes en Europe orientale. Ici, des juifs polonais posant, vers 1900.

Traditional ways of life included traditional ways of earning a living. Few worked harder than the women of the ancient Copenhagen fish market, Denmark, 1906. Food supply to big cities was still largely in the hands of individuals.

Eine traditionelle Lebensweise bedeutete auch, seinen Lebensunterhalt auf traditionelle Weise zu verdienen. Kaum jemand arbeitete härter als die Frauen auf dem alten Fischmarkt in Kopenhagen, Dänemark, 1906. Die Versorgung großer Städte mit Lebensmitteln lag zu weiten Teilen noch in den Händen von Privatpersonen.

Les modes de vie traditionnels comprenaient aussi des métiers traditionnels. Peu de gens travaillaient plus dur que les femmes de l'ancien marché au poisson de Copenhague, Danemark, 1906. L'approvisionnement en nourriture des grandes villes était assumé en grande partie par les individus.

By the beginning of the 20th century, most Native Americans had been driven from their lands and forced to adopt the white man's ways.

Anfang des 20. Jahrhunderts waren viele Ureinwohner Amerikas von ihrem Land vertrieben worden. Man zwang ihnen die Lebensweise des weißen Mannes auf.

Au début du XXᵉ siècle, la plupart des Indiens d'Amérique avaient été chassés de leurs terres et forcés d'adopter le mode de vie des Blancs.

Some – such as
Show As He Goes
(opposite) and this
young Hopi mother
and child (right) –
were photographed
by Edward S Curtis
as part of a lasting
record of a fast-
disappearing culture.

Einige dieser
Ureinwohner –
wie zum Beispiel
Show As He Goes
(gegenüberliegende
Seite) und diese junge
Hopi-Mutter mit
ihrem Kind (rechts) –
wurden von Edward
S. Curtis als Teil
einer bleibenden
Dokumentation einer
rasch untergehenden
Kultur fotografiert.

Certains – comme
Show As He Goes
(Vois-celui-qui-
marche) (ci-contre)
ou cette jeune mère
hopi et son enfant
(à droite) – furent
photographiés par
Edward S. Curtis,
dont l'œuvre consista
à fixer les traces
d'une civilisation en
train de disparaître.

Technically free. A generation after the abolition of slavery in
the United States, the average black American lived barely above
subsistence level. This family was photographed in Oklahoma
in 1901.

Theoretisch frei. Eine Generation nach der Abschaffung der Skla-
verei in den Vereinigten Staaten. Der durchschnittliche schwarze
Amerikaner lebte nur knapp über dem Existenzminimum. Diese
Familie wurde in Oklahoma im Jahr 1901 fotografiert.

Liberté formelle. Une génération après l'abolition de l'esclavage aux
États-Unis, l'Américain noir moyen vivait à peine au-dessus du seuil
de la misère. Cette famille fut photographiée en Oklahoma en 1901.

Technologically enslaved. However bad life was for the black American, it was worse for the average African. Slavery and vicious cruelty were a way of life in many European colonies. (Above) A group of slaves is guarded by an Ashanti soldier.

Praktisch versklavt. So schlecht das Leben der schwarzen Amerikaner auch war, für den durchschnittlichen Afrikaner war es weitaus schlechter. Sklaverei und brutale Misshandlungen waren in vielen europäischen Kolonien an der Tagesordnung. (Oben) Eine Gruppe von Sklaven wird von einem Ashanti-Soldaten bewacht.

Esclavage réel. Si la vie était difficile pour les Noirs d'Amérique, elle était pire encore pour l'Africain moyen. Dans de nombreuses colonies européennes, l'esclavage, les mauvais traitements et les cruautés étaient leur lot quotidien. (Ci-dessus) Un groupe d'esclaves sous la garde d'un soldat ashanti.

Old-style law. Headmen of the Tlingit tribe of the north-west coast of America. The elaborate blankets worn by two of the men, called Chilkat blankets, were traditionally woven from cedar bark and mountain goat's wool and would be worn for a potlatch.

Das Gesetz der Ahnen. Häuptlinge vom Stamm der Tlingit an der Nordwestküste Amerikas. Die kunstvoll gefertigten Decken (so genannte Chilkat-Decken), die zwei Männer tragen, wurden traditionell aus Zedernrinde und Bergziegenwolle gewebt. Sie wurden bei Potlatch-Zeremonien getragen.

La loi ancestrale. Les chefs de la tribu des Tlingit, sur la côte nord-ouest américaine. Les couvertures très travaillées, appelées chilkat, que portent deux d'entre eux, étaient traditionnellement tissées à partir d'écorce de cèdre et de laine de chèvres des montagnes. On les portait lors d'un potlatch (fête où l'on échange des cadeaux).

New-style law. Judge Henry H Campbell is master of all he surveys on the Matador Ranch, Texas, 1908 (photograph by Erwin E Smith). The problem was that much of what he surveyed was harsh scrubland, and even his own cabin was far from prepossessing.

Das Gesetz der neuen Zeit. Der Richter Henry H. Campbell ist Herr über alles, was er auf der Matador-Ranch überblicken kann, Texas, 1908 (aufgenommen von Erwin E. Smith). Das meiste aber, was er erblicken konnte, war leider nur stoppeliges Buschland. Selbst seine eigene Hütte sah alles andere als verlockend aus.

La loi des temps modernes. Le juge Henry H. Campbell était le propriétaire de toutes les terres qu'il pouvait embrasser du regard (photo par Erwin E. Smith). Le problème était que cela représentait à peine davantage qu'une terre de broussailles aride ; et sa cabane n'avait rien de luxueux.

There was little left of the world that was unexplored, but in the far north of the American continent there were still vast wildernesses of which little was known. These Canadian Native Americans of the Subarctic were trappers, hunters and fishermen.

Nur wenige Gebiete der Welt waren noch nicht erschlossen, doch im hohen Norden Amerikas gab es noch eine riesige, nahezu unbekannte Wildnis. Diese kanadischen Ureinwohner der Subarktis waren Trapper, Jäger und Fischer.

Peu de territoires restaient inexplorés dans le monde, mais il subsistait dans l'extrême nord du continent américain de grandes étendues sauvages dont on ignorait presque tout. Les Indiens des régions subarctiques du Canada étaient des trappeurs, des chasseurs et des pêcheurs.

Although this Alaskan hut of 1900 was said to be a great improvement on the more traditional dwellings of the indigenous natives of Yakutat Bay, the photographer noted: 'The dull, stupid or resigned look on their faces… appears to be the result of contact with civilisation.'

Obwohl diese Hütte in Alaska von 1900 als eine große Verbesserung gegenüber den traditionellen Behausungen der einheimischen Bewohner der Yakutatbai galt, bemerkte der Fotograf: „Der gelangweilte, stumpfe und resignierte Ausdruck in ihren Gesichtern … scheint zu zeigen, dass sie mit der Zivilisation in Kontakt gekommen waren."

Comparée aux demeures traditionnelles des habitants de Yakutat Bay, cette baraque en Alaska était considérée comme un progrès, 1900. Pourtant le photographe nota : « L'air borné, stupide et résigné qui est sur leur visage … semble bien être le résultat de leurs contacts avec la civilisation ».

Little more than twenty years had passed since the war in which a British army had been annihilated by Zulu impis at Isandhlwana in 1879. Their teeth drawn, the Zulus shown here are almost certainly carrying ceremonial or dance regalia rather than weapons of war.

Kaum mehr als 20 Jahre waren seit dem Krieg vergangen, in dem eine britische Armee von den Zulu bei Isandhlwana im Jahre 1879 vernichtend geschlagen worden war. Die hier abgebildeten Zulu tragen wahrscheinlich eher rituelle beziehungsweise tänzerische Insignien und keine Kriegswaffen.

À peine plus de 20 ans s'étaient écoulés depuis la guerre où une armée britannique avait été écrasée par des guerriers zoulous à Isandhlwana en 1879. Les Zoulous photographiés ici portent très vraisemblablement des atours de cérémonie ou de danse plutôt que des armes de guerre.

In the wake of the armies of the West trudged the photographers, the anthropologists and the newly emerging social scientists. They recorded houses, tools, implements and – especially – people, such as these young Zulu women of 1900.

Den westlichen Armeen folgten die Fotografen, Anthropologen und Sozialwissenschaftler, die zu der Zeit gerade in Erscheinung traten. Sie machten Aufnahmen von Häusern, Werkzeugen, Gerätschaften und insbesondere von Menschen wie diesen jungen Zulufrauen aus dem Jahre 1900.

Les armées occidentales entraînèrent dans leur sillage des photographes, des anthropologues et des chercheurs en sciences sociales, lesquelles venaient de naître. Ils photographiaient les maisons, les outils, les équipements et surtout les gens, comme ces jeunes femmes zouloues de 1900.

4. Migration
Ein- und Auswanderung
Les migrations

Beset with a mixture of hope, anxiety and bewilderment, a young immigrant arrives at Ellis Island, New York, in 1905. By this time more than 100,000 religious, political and economic refugees were sailing from Europe to the United States every year.

Mit gemischten Gefühlen, voller Hoffnung, Angst und Verwirrung kommt eine junge Einwanderin auf Ellis Island an, New York, 1905. Bis zu diesem Zeitpunkt waren jedes Jahr mehr als 100 000 Glaubens-, Wirtschafts- und politische Flüchtlinge mit dem Schiff von Europa in die Vereinigten Staaten gereist.

Animée d'un mélange d'espoir, d'inquiétude et de confusion, une jeune immigrée débarque à Ellis Island, à New York, en 1905. À cette époque, plus de 100 000 réfugiés politiques, religieux ou économiques quittaient chaque année l'Europe pour les États-Unis.

4. Migration
Ein- und Auswanderung
Les migrations

They came by ship – from China to California, from India to Africa, from Europe to the eastern seaboard of the United States. Few of them came of their own free will, for they were driven by desperation. They were desperate for freedom, work or both. They had heard of new lands and new opportunities, of cities where the old prejudices and bigotry did not exist, of virgin land unbroken by the plough. They had also heard of streets paved with gold, of earth so rich and fecund that crops grew from seed to maturity in the space of a few days, of rocks that spewed forth jewels and the ore of precious metals by the barrow-load.

Their courage matched their naïvety. They braved storms at sea in vessels scarcely strong enough to withstand the waves of thousands of miles of ocean. They risked the strong possibility of rejection at the end of their journeys and an immediate return to the land whence they came. For the lands that summoned the destitute and the homeless had no welcome for the physically frail or the politically unsound.

But still they came in their hundreds of thousands, becoming the new citizens of new nations, bringing with them old cultures, old skills and, in a few, sad cases, old prejudices.

Sie kamen mit dem Schiff – von China nach Kalifornien, von Indien nach Afrika, von Europa an die Ostküste der Vereinigten Staaten. Nur wenige kamen aus freien Stücken, die meisten wurden von der Verzweiflung getrieben. Freiheit, Arbeit, oder auch beides zugleich, das war ihre Sehnsucht. Sie hatten von neuen Welten und ungeahnten Möglichkeiten gehört, von Städten, in denen die alten Vorurteile und die Engstirnigkeit aufgehoben waren, und von noch nicht erschlossenem Neuland. Sie hatten von mit Gold gepflasterten Straßen gehört, von Böden, die so reich und fruchtbar waren, dass die Ernte innerhalb weniger Tage reifte, und von Felsen, aus denen Edelsteine und -metalle hervorquollen.

Ihr Mut war genauso groß wie ihre Naivität. Tapfer überstanden sie die Stürme auf Schiffen, die kaum stabil genug waren, den Wellen über Tausende von Seemeilen standzuhalten. Sie gingen das hohe Risiko ein, am Ende ihrer Reise möglicherweise abgewiesen zu werden und sofort wieder in das Land, aus dem sie gekommen waren, zurückgeschickt zu werden. Denn die Länder, von denen die armen und heimatlosen Menschen angezogen waren, empfingen die körperlich schwachen und die politisch aufsässigen Leute nicht mit offenen Armen.

Dennoch kamen sie zu Hunderttausenden und wurden die neuen Bürger der neuen Nationen – die gleichzeitig alte Kulturen, alte Fertigkeiten und, in einigen bedauerlichen Fällen, auch alte Vorurteile mitbrachten.

Ils voyageaient par bateaux de Chine en Californie, d'Inde en Afrique, d'Europe à la côte est des États-Unis. Peu d'entre eux venaient de leur plein gré, car ils étaient poussés par le désespoir. Ils étaient désespérément en quête de liberté, de travail, ou des deux. Ils avaient entendu parler d'un pays jeune et de possibilités neuves, de villes où les préjugés anciens et la bigoterie n'existaient pas, de terres vierges encore jamais labourées. Ils avaient aussi entendu parler de rues pavées d'or, d'une terre si riche et si féconde que les moissons jaillissaient et passaient en quelques jours à peine du germe à la maturité, de roches qui crachaient diamants et métaux précieux par pleines charretées.

Leur courage n'avait d'égal que leur naïveté. Ils avaient bravé des tempêtes en mer, dans des bateaux à peine assez résistants pour tenir contre les vagues pendant les milliers de miles de la traversée. Ils prenaient le risque réel d'être refoulés au terme de leur voyage et de devoir reprendre immédiatement la mer pour rentrer chez eux. En effet, ces pays qui appelaient les pauvres et les sans-patrie n'accueillaient ni les santés précaires, ni les engagements suspects.

Malgré cela, ils débarquaient par centaines de milliers. Ils devinrent les nouveaux citoyens de nouvelles nations, apportant avec eux leur culture ancestrale, leurs savoir-faire traditionnels et dans certains cas hélas, leurs vieux préjugés aussi.

A Polish emigrant
boards the
SS *General Grant* –
the last leg in
a journey of hope
to the New World.

Ein polnischer
Auswanderer geht
an Bord des
Dampfschiffes
SS *General Grant* –
die letzte Etappe auf
einer Reise voller
Hoffnung in die
Neue Welt.

Un Polonais
monte à bord du
SS *General Grant* –
dernière étape d'un
voyage plein
d'espoir vers le
Nouveau Monde.

Emigrants crowd together on the deck of the White Star Company liner *Westernland*, sailing from Antwerp to New York. Their journey may have begun months earlier, in a horse-drawn cart or on foot, trudging from east to west across Europe.

Auswanderer sitzen dicht gedrängt auf dem Deck des Liniendampfers *Westernland* der White Star Company auf dem Weg von Antwerpen nach New York. Ihre Reise hatte möglicherweise schon mehrere Monate zuvor begonnen, auf einem Pferdewagen oder zu Fuß von Ost nach West quer durch Europa.

Des émigrants entassés sur le pont du *Westernland,* de la compagnie maritime White Star, au départ d'Anvers pour New York. Leur voyage a sans doute commencé des mois auparavant, soit à pied, soit dans une carriole tirée par un cheval, traversant péniblement l'Europe d'est en ouest.

(Opposite) Immigrants begin the 'processing' at Ellis Island.
(Right) An elderly Jew gazes out at a new Promised Land.

(Gegenüberliegende Seite) Einwanderer bei ihrer „Abfertigung" auf Ellis Island.
(Rechts) Ein älterer Jude hält Ausschau nach einem neuen „Gelobten Land".

(Ci-contre) Des émigrés entament la procédure d'admission à Ellis Island.
(À droite) Un vieux juif contemple une nouvelle Terre promise.

The Registry Hall on Ellis Island, 1905. Penned in like cattle, the immigrants waited for their numbers to be called. Their real names were often abandoned by officials unable to distinguish names from destinations as pronounced by the new arrivals.

Die Meldehalle auf Ellis Island, 1905. Eingepfercht wie in einem Viehstall warteten die Einwanderer darauf, dass ihre Nummern aufgerufen wurden. Die Beamten verzichteten oftmals auf die richtigen Namen der Einwanderer, da sie diese in der Aussprache der Neuankömmlinge nicht von den Reisezielen unterscheiden konnten.

Le hall d'enregistrement à Ellis Island, 1905. Parqués comme du bétail, les émigrés attendaient d'être appelés par un numéro. Leurs noms étaient souvent modifiés par des fonctionnaires incapables de distinguer les noms de personnes des noms de destinations, déformés par la prononciation des nouveaux arrivants.

A customs official attaches labels to the coats of a German immigrant family in the Registry Hall, 1905. Most families managed to keep together, for there was no rush and no panic – only the dreadful fear of rejection and summary return to Europe.

Ein Zollbeamter befestigt kleine Schilder auf den Mänteln einer deutschen Einwandererfamilie in der Meldehalle, 1905. Den meisten Familien gelang es, zusammenzubleiben, denn es herrschte weder Eile noch Panik. Sie hatten nur furchtbare Angst, abgewiesen und sofort wieder nach Europa zurückgeschickt zu werden.

Un fonctionnaire des douanes attache des étiquettes aux manteaux des membres d'une famille d'émigrés allemands dans le hall d'enregistrement, 1905. La plupart des familles réussissaient à rester ensemble, car il n'y avait ni bousculade ni panique – seulement la terrible peur d'être refoulés et renvoyés en Europe sans autre procès.

The moment
of truth – new
immigrants are
inspected for signs
of disease, c. 1900.
Fail this test and
there was no hope
of entry into the
United States.

Die Stunde der
Wahrheit – neu
angekommene Ein-
wanderer werden
auf Krankheiten
untersucht, um
1900. Fiel diese
Untersuchung
negativ aus, war
eine Einreise in die
Vereinigten Staaten
hoffnungslos.

Le moment de
vérité. Les candidats
à l'immigration
subissent un examen
destiné à révéler
d'éventuelles
maladies, vers 1900.
Échouer à ce test
vous enlevait tout
espoir d'entrer aux
États-Unis.

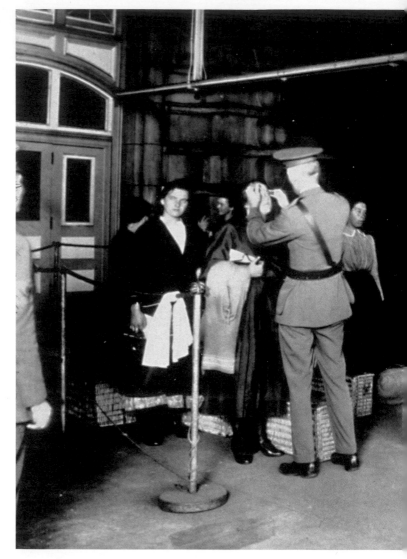

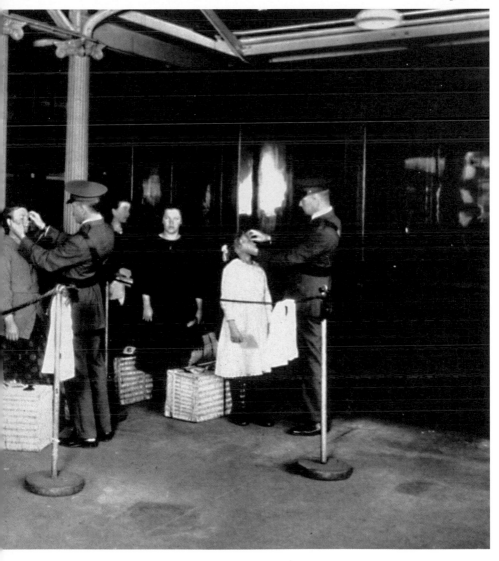

Jewish emigrants from England await inspection at Ellis Island, c. 1900. There were two doors leading from the main building. One led to boats for the short crossing to New York City. The other – for the unsuccessful – led to ships for the long journey back to Europe.

Jüdische Auswanderer aus England kurz vor ihrer Untersuchung auf Ellis Island, um 1900. Es gab zwei Ausgangstüren im Hauptgebäude. Die eine führte zu Booten für die kurze Überfahrt nach New York City. Die andere – für die Abgewiesenen – führte zu den Schiffen für die lange Rückreise nach Europa.

Des émigrés juifs anglais attendant l'inspection à Ellis Island, vers 1900. Le bâtiment principal possédait deux portes de sortie. L'une conduisait aux bateaux qui assuraient la brève traversée vers la ville de New York. L'autre – pour les moins chanceux – menait aux navires qui repartaient pour le long voyage vers l'Europe.

Jakob Mithelstadt, his wife and family, newly arrived from Russia on the SS *Pretoria*, await permission to proceed to Kulm, North Dakota. Often, immigrants arrived with a single name scribbled on a piece of paper. Sometimes it was their own, sometimes that of their destination.

Jakob Mithelstadt mit seiner Frau und seinen Kindern. Sie sind gerade mit dem Dampfschiff SS *Pretoria* aus Russland angekommen. Sie warten auf die Erlaubnis, ihren Weg nach Kulm, North Dakota, fortsetzen zu können. Häufig kamen die Einwanderer mit einem einzigen, auf ein kleines Stück Papier gekritzelten Namen an. Manchmal war es ihr eigener Name, manchmal der ihres Reiseziels.

Jakob Mithelstadt, sa femme et leurs enfants, tout juste arrivés de Russie sur le SS *Pretoria*, attendent la permission de se rendre à Kulm, dans le nord du Dakota. Les émigrés arrivaient souvent avec un simple nom griffoné sur un bout de papier. Parfois c'était le leur, parfois celui de leur destination.

A group of Italian immigrants in the waiting hall at Ellis Island. Most Italians headed straight for New York, Chicago or another large city. There was plenty of work in the sweatshops of New York's Little Italy.

Eine Gruppe italienischer Einwanderer in der Wartehalle auf Ellis Island. Die meisten Italiener zog es direkt nach New York, Chicago oder in eine andere Großstadt. In den Ausbeuterbetrieben von Little Italy in New York gab es reichlich Arbeit.

Un groupe d'émigrés italiens dans la salle d'attente d'Ellis Island. La plupart des Italiens se rendaient directement à New York, à Chicago ou dans une autre grande ville. Il y avait abondance de travail dans les ateliers clandestins du quartier de Little Italy, à New York.

Italian immigrants
at Ellis Island, 1905.
It is unlikely that
the luggage in the
background belongs
to them.

Italienische Ein-
wanderer auf Ellis
Island, 1905. Es ist
unwahrscheinlich,
dass ihnen das
Gepäck im Hinter-
grund gehörte.

Des émigrés italiens
à Ellis Island, 1905.
Il est peu vraisem-
blable que les
bagages qui sont
derrière eux leur
appartiennent.

The pushcart market in the East Side ghetto of New York, 1900. This was the centre of the Jewish quarter. Newly-arrived Jews headed here for the newspaper offices which served as property and employment agencies and marriage bureaux.

Der Handkarrenmarkt im Ghetto auf der East Side von New York, 1900. Dies war das Zentrum des jüdischen Viertels. Jüdische Neuankömmlinge steuerten hier direkt die Zeitungsredaktionen an, die als Maklerbüros, Arbeits- und Heiratsvermittlungen dienten.

Les charrettes à bras du marché dans le ghetto de l'East-Side, New York, 1900. C'était le cœur du quartier juif. Les juifs nouvellement arrivés venaient tout droit ici, dans des bureaux de presse qui servaient en même temps d'agences immobilières, de bureaux de placement et d'agences matrimoniales.

An immigrant family in a New York slum, 1900. After a journey of several thousand miles, this one-room hovel was their new home. It was also the beginning of a new life, and, it was to be hoped, an end to persecution.

Eine Einwandererfamilie in einem Elendsviertel von New York, 1900. Nach einer mehrere tausend Meilen langen Reise war dieses armselige Zimmer ihr neues Zuhause. Auch war es der Beginn eines neuen Lebens und, so hofften sie, ein Ende der Verfolgung.

Une famille d'émigrés dans un taudis new-yorkais, 1900. Au bout d'un voyage de plusieurs milliers de kilomètres, cette pièce misérable est leur nouvelle maison. C'est aussi le début d'une nouvelle vie et l'espoir de la fin des persécutions.

5.   Haves and have-nots
   Arm und Reich
   Les nantis et les démunis

Rich and poor were united in their attitudes to taxation. The rich
had been assaulted and insulted by the death duties imposed by
the Liberal Government on large estates; the poor were more
concerned with the threatened bread tax at the end of the decade.

Die Armen und die Reichen waren einer Meinung, wenn es um
die Besteuerung ging. Die liberale Regierung war über die Reichen
hergefallen und hatte sie mit den Erbschaftssteuern auf große
Vermögen zutiefst getroffen. Die Armen waren am Ende dieses
Jahrzehnts eher von der drohenden Brotsteuer betroffen.

Riches et pauvres étaient d'accord pour rejeter les impôts. Les
riches avaient eu à souffrir de l'imposition très brutale décrétée
par le gouvernement libéral sur les grandes fortunes ; les pauvres
étaient plus concernés par la taxe sur le pain qui menaçait vers
la fin de la décennie.

5. Haves and have-nots
Arm und Reich
Les nantis et les démunis

It is temptingly easy to romanticise the past, to exaggerate the quality of life of both rich and poor in the 1900s. Certainly, the poor were often ill-housed, ill-fed or just plain ill, but their lives were in many ways considerably better than they had been 50 or 60 years earlier. In all but the newest industrial nations there was legislation to limit hours of work and the worst excesses of exploitation. There were inspectors of factories and mines. There were bodies empowered to check the purity of the public water supply, to oversee education for all, to exercise some control over town and city development.

For all that, the poor still suffered extreme hardship. Social welfare schemes were in their infancy. Private charities offered patchwork care. It was hard for do-gooders to keep pace with the brash inventiveness of exploitation. There was little to stop the publican watering the workers' beer, the grocer from falsifying his scales, the landlord from over-crowding his slum tenements.

And, for all that, the rich did live in luxury and style beyond imagination. There was precious little room on the ladder that led from one class to another.

Man neigt dazu, die Vergangenheit zu romantisieren und die Lebensqualität der Reichen und der Armen zu Beginn des 20. Jahrhunderts zu beschönigen. Sicher wohnten die Armen häufig in schlechten Behausungen, hatten keine gute Ernährung oder waren schwer krank, doch ihr Leben war bedeutend besser als 50 oder 60 Jahre zuvor. In fast allen Industrienationen gab es gesetzliche Beschränkungen der Arbeitszeit und übermäßiger Ausbeutung. Fabriken und Bergwerke wurden überwacht. Befugte Organe überprüften die öffentliche Wasserversorgung, beaufsichtigten die Bildung und Erziehung für jedermann und kontrollierten in gewissem Maße die Stadtentwicklung.

Dennoch litten die Armen immer noch äußerst große Not. Sozialhilfeprogramme steckten noch in den Kinderschuhen. Private Wohltätigkeitsvereine boten hier und da Hilfe an. Für die Weltverbesserer war es schwer, mit dem unverfrorenen Einfallsreichtum der Ausbeuter Schritt zu halten. Man konnte den Gastwirten kaum Einhalt gebieten, wenn sie das Bier für die Arbeiter mit Wasser panschten. Auch den Lebensmittelhändler, der seine Waage falsch eichte, und den Vermieter, der zu viele Menschen in seine Mietshäuser in den Elendsvierteln aufnahm, konnte man kaum daran hindern.

Die Reichen lebten trotz alledem in unvorstellbarem Luxus und Überfluss. Überdies war auf der gesellschaftlichen Leiter, die von einer sozialen Stufe zur nächsten führte, herzlich wenig Platz.

Il est toujours tentant et facile d'idéaliser le passé, d'exagérer la qualité de la vie des riches comme d'ailleurs celle des nécessiteux, dans les années 1900. Sans doute, les pauvres étaient souvent mal logés, mal nourris ou tout simplement malades mais, sous de nombreux aspects, leurs conditions de vie étaient meilleures qu'elles ne l'avaient été 50 ou 60 ans auparavant. Dans tous les pays dont l'industrialisation était déjà ancienne, la législation limitait les heures de travail et les plus graves excès de l'exploitation. Les usines et les mines étaient régulièrement inspectées. Il existait des institutions chargées de vérifier la pureté de l'eau du service public, d'assurer l'éducation pour tous, de contrôler le développement urbain.

Pour autant, les difficultés des plus pauvres restaient extrêmes. Les programmes sociaux étaient encore dans les limbes. La charité privée colmatait les brèches, tant bien que mal. Il était difficile pour les philanthropes de réussir à tenir le rythme des exploiteurs, jamais à court d'inventivité ni d'audace. Peu de choses pouvaient empêcher le bistrotier de couper d'eau la bière des ouvriers, l'épicier de fausser sa balance, le propriétaire de surpeupler ses taudis.

À côté de cela, les riches vivaient dans un luxe et une profusion qui dépassaient l'imagination. Il existait cependant quelques barreaux intermédiaires très recherchés sur l'échelle conduisant d'une classe à l'autre.

Families were often thrown out onto the street with their possessions. Eviction, in London and elsewhere, was a common fate and a constant nightmare for those who were unable to pay their rent. Casual workers – dockers, labourers and the unskilled – were the worst hit.

Familien wurden häufig mit ihrem ganzen Hab und Gut auf die Straße gesetzt. Wohnungs-räumungen in London und anderswo waren ein weit verbreitetes Schicksal und ein ständiger Alptraum für diejenigen, die ihre Miete nicht bezahlen konnten. Gelegenheitsarbeiter – wie Hafenarbeiter, Tagelöhner und Hilfsarbeiter – waren davon am schlimmsten betroffen.

Des familles étaient souvent jetées à la rue avec leurs biens. À Londres comme ailleurs, les expulsions étaient courantes et devenaient le cauchemar de ceux qui ne parvenaient pas à payer leur loyer. Les travailleurs journaliers – dockers, manœuvres et ouvriers non-qualifiés – étaient le plus durement frappés.

Home was often a single room where all the family lived, worked and sometimes died. The luxury of a weekly bath from a basin by the fire was denied many; most went to the public baths or remained dirty.

Das Zuhause bestand für viele nur aus einem einzigen Raum, in dem die ganze Familie lebte, arbeitete und manchmal auch starb. Der Luxus, einmal in der Woche ein Bad in einer Waschschüssel neben dem Ofen zu nehmen, war vielen versagt. Die meisten gingen in öffentliche Badehäuser oder blieben einfach dreckig.

Le foyer était parfois une simple chambre où vivait, travaillait et parfois mourait toute une famille. Le luxe d'un bain hebdomadaire dans une bassine près du feu était refusé à beaucoup ; la plupart des gens avaient le choix entre les bains publics et rester sales.

In a life that threatened to be eaten away by misery, there were few means of escape. One (opposite) was a shot of morphine. Another – cheaper and longer lasting – was sleep. (Above) Vagrants doze on a bench in St James's Park, London, October 1900.

Es gab nur wenige Möglichkeiten, einem vom Elend gezeichneten Leben zu entkommen. Eine davon (gegenüberliegende Seite) war ein Schuss Morphium. Eine andere – billiger und dauerhafter – war der Schlaf. (Oben) Stadtstreicher machen ein Nickerchen auf einer Parkbank im St. James's Park, London, Oktober 1900.

Lorsque la vie menaçait d'être rongée par la misère, il y avait peu de moyens de s'évader. L'un de ces moyens (ci-contre) était la morphine. Un autre – moins cher et plus durable – était le sommeil. (Ci-dessus) Des vagabonds dorment sur un banc à St James's Park, Londres, octobre 1900.

A few streets away life could be immeasurably better. Even a moderate income was enough for a large house, servants, holidays at the seaside, and a walled garden. This Edwardian family enjoys the garden in the summer of 1905.

Nur ein paar Straßen weiter konnte das Leben sehr viel besser sein. Sogar ein durchschnittliches Einkommen reichte für ein großes Haus, Bedienstete, Urlaub am Meer und einen von einer Mauer umgebenen Garten. Zur Zeit Edwards VII. vergnügt sich diese Familie im Sommer 1905 in ihrem Garten.

À quelques rues de distance à peine, la vie pouvait être d'une douceur incommensurable. Un revenu moyen suffisait parfois pour entretenir une grande maison, des domestiques, un jardin entouré de hauts murs et passer les vacances à la mer. Sous le règne d'Édouard VII, une famille profitant de son jardin, pendant l'été de 1905.

This family, taking tea in 1909, is not particularly wealthy. The tablecloth is limp and slightly stained, and the children – despite their Eton collars – are not smartly dressed. But the ornaments, the bookshelves and the tea service indicate they are comfortable enough.

Diese Familie, hier beim Tee im Jahre 1909, ist nicht besonders wohlhabend. Das Tischtuch ist nicht gestärkt und leicht fleckig. Die Kinder – trotz ihrer breiten Umlegekragen – sind nicht sehr vornehm gekleidet. Doch die Ziergegenstände, die Bücherregale und das Teeservice deuten darauf hin, dass sie in relativem Wohlstand leben.

Cette famille qui prend le thé en 1909 n'est pas spécialement riche. La nappe est usée et quelque peu tachée et en dépit de leurs grands cols durs, les enfants ne sont pas bien habillés. Mais les décorations, les armoires à livres et le service à thé indiquent une relative aisance.

If you sought real comfort, it was better to be rich and male. However wealthy,
a woman's place was in the home, a man's in his club. Hock and seltzer lads of
the early 1900s meet to smoke and drink.

Suchte man den wahren Komfort, war es besser, reich und männlich zu sein.
Unabhängig von ihrem Wohlstand war der Platz einer Frau im Haus, der eines
Mannes in seinem Club. Freunde von weißem Rheinwein und Selterswasser treffen
sich in gemütlicher Runde zum Rauchen und Trinken Anfang des 20. Jahrhunderts.

Pour jouir réellement des agréments de la vie, il valait mieux être riche, et homme.
Si grande que fût son aisance matérielle, la place d'une femme était à la maison,
tandis que celle de l'homme était à son club. Quelques bons vivants de la bonne
société, réunis pour boire et fumer, au début des années 1900.

There were plenty of clubs for gentlemen, in town and country. Among the increasingly popular were sporting clubs. This is the 19th Hole at the fashionable Ranelagh Golf Club, near London, c. 1900.

Die Anzahl der Herrenclubs in der Stadt und auf dem Lande war groß. Sportclubs erfreuten sich damals immer größerer Beliebtheit. Dies ist das Clubzimmer „19. Loch" im vornehmen Ranelagh Golf Club in der Nähe von London, um 1900.

Il existait un nombre incalculable de clubs pour gentlemen, en ville et à la campagne. Les clubs de sport étaient particulièrement appréciés. Ici, le « 19ᵉ trou » au très huppé Ranelagh Golf Club, près de Londres, vers 1900.

A family in a London slum, 1901. Philanthropists throughout the West were doing what they could to improve housing for the poor, but the vast majority still lived in slums that were dark, dangerous, cold in winter and stifling in summer.

Eine Familie in einem Londoner Elendsviertel, 1901. Philanthropen taten überall in der westlichen Welt, was in ihrer Macht stand, um die Unterkünfte der Armen zu verbessern. Doch der Großteil der Armen lebte immer noch in Elendsvierteln, die dunkel, gefährlich, im Winter kalt und im Sommer stickig waren.

Une famille dans un taudis de Londres, 1901. Un peu partout en Europe, les philanthropes faisaient ce qu'ils pouvaient pour améliorer les conditions de logement des démunis, mais la grande majorité vivait malgré cela dans des habitations froides, obscures et mal protégées en hiver, suffocantes en été.

An idyllic outing for all ages and both sexes – a picnic party at Netley Abbey, Hampshire, in the summer of 1900. The picnickers almost certainly travelled to the Abbey by horse-drawn charabanc.

Ein idyllischer Ausflug für jedermann und jederfrau jeden Alters – ein Picknickvergnügen bei der Klosterkirche Netley Abbey, Hampshire, im Sommer 1900. Die Ausflugler fuhren höchstwahrscheinlich mit einem Pferdeomnibus zu dieser Klosterkirche.

Un déjeuner de campagne idyllique pour tous les âges et les deux sexes : pique-nique à Netley Abbey, dans le Hampshire, au cours de l'été 1900. Les participants s'étaient sûrement rendus à l'abbaye dans une carriole tirée par des chevaux.

The claustrophobic clutter of the Victorian parlour gave way to the simpler lines of Edwardian furnishing (above). The responsibility for dusting every ornament and every shelf – as well as a hundred other jobs – fell on the maid (opposite).

Das überladene Durcheinander der viktorianischen Salons wurde von den geraderen Linien der Möbel aus der Zeit Edwards VII. abgelöst (oben). Das Abstauben aller Ziergegenstände und Regale sowie viele weitere Aufgaben fielen dem Hausmädchen zu (gegenüberliegende Seite).

Le fouillis claustrophobique du petit salon victorien avait cédé la place aux lignes plus simples du mobilier édouardien (ci-dessus). L'époussetage de tous les ornements et de chaque étagère ainsi que des centaines d'autres responsabilités incombaient à la bonne (ci-contre).

As well as free handouts of bread and soup, the unemployed and the homeless
in New York could visit the Bowery Mission for free cups of coffee. This
picture was taken in February 1908 – a time when the American economy
was booming.

Zusätzlich zu der kostenlosen Ausgabe von Brot und Suppe konnten die
Arbeitslosen und Obdachlosen in New York bei der Bowery Mission umsonst
Kaffee trinken. Dieses Foto wurde im Februar 1908 aufgenommen – in einer
Zeit, in der die amerikanische Wirtschaft boomte.

Les chômeurs et les sans-abri de New York pouvaient trouver du pain, de la
soupe ou encore du café gratuits à la Bowery Mission. Cette photo fut prise
en février 1908, à une époque où l'économie américaine était en plein essor.

Across the other side of the world, 'Grand Russians' – in this case merchants from Nijni-Novgorod – take tea, 29 August 1905. The surroundings may look a little sparse, but the tea set and the samovar are most impressive.

Auf der anderen Seite der Erdkugel: „Vornehme" Russen – hier Kaufleute aus Nishnij Nowgorod – beim Tee, 29. August 1905. Die Umgebung mag ein wenig ärmlich erscheinen, doch sind das Teeservice und der Samowar sehr beeindruckend.

À l'autre bout du monde, des « Grands-Russes », ici des marchands de Nijni-Novgorod, boivent le thé, 29 août 1905. Le cadre peut sembler un peu austère, mais le service à thé et le samovar sont très impressionnants.

Stuffed shirts. Friends and colleagues of Richmond Keele in their serried
ranks at a dinner in his honour at the Café Royal, London, 20 October
1903. The amount of cutlery on the tables suggests they are in for a 'beano'.

Voll gestopfte Wichtigtuer. Freunde und Kollegen sitzen zu Ehren von
Richmond Keele in eng geschlossenen Reihen beim Abendessen im Café
Royal, London, 20. Oktober 1903. Die Menge an Besteck auf den Tischen
lässt vermuten, dass sie auf einen „großen Schmaus" warten.

Plastrons rebondis. Des amis et collègues de Richmond Keele en rangs
serrés lors d'un dîner en son honneur au Café Royal de Londres,
20 octobre 1903. Le couvert nombreux sur les tables semble promettre
bombance.

Empty bellies. A couple of miles away, on the same night, the benches of the Salvation Army shelter for the homeless of Blackfriars would have been crowded. The poor were best kept off the streets, where they might have caused mischief.

Leere Bäuche. Nur einige Kilometer weiter am selben Abend waren die Bänke im Obdachlosenheim der Heilsarmee in Blackfriars überfüllt. Die Armen sollten am besten von der Straße ferngehalten werden, wo sie ihr Unwesen hätten treiben können.

Ventres creux. Quelques kilomètres plus loin, le même soir, les bancs du refuge pour sans-abri de l'Armée du Salut de Blackfriars affichent complet. On évitait de laisser les pauvres dans les rues, par crainte d'éventuels méfaits.

A meeting place for rich and poor. Paul Martin's photograph shows a bootblack polishing the shoes of a London gentleman, c. 1900. The plinth behind the bootblack suggests that the scene is somewhere in the City of London.

Ein Treffpunkt für Arm und Reich. Das Foto von Paul Martin zeigt einen Schuhputzer bei seiner Arbeit. Er poliert die Schuhe eines Londoner Gentlemans, um 1900. Die Plinthe (Säulenplatte) hinter dem Schuhputzer deutet darauf hin, dass sich diese Szene irgendwo im Stadtzentrum von London abspielt.

Un lieu qui réunit riches et pauvres. Cette photo de Paul Martin montre un cireur s'affairant à lustrer les chaussures d'un gentleman londonien, vers 1900. Le socle dont on voit un bout derrière le cireur indique que la scène se passe quelque part dans la City de Londres.

And meanwhile, well to the east, a more humble bootblack cleans the shoes of a less smart customer. In an age when there was far more mud and dust on the city streets, shoes needed cleaning more often than they do today.

Derweil putzt ganz im Osten der Stadt ein eher bescheidener Schuhputzer die Schuhe eines weniger vornehmen Kunden. In einer Zeit, als es noch viel mehr Schmutz und Staub auf den Straßen in der Stadt gab, mussten die Schuhe öfter geputzt werden als heutzutage.

Pendant ce temps, beaucoup plus loin à l'est, un cireur moins stylé nettoie les chaussures d'un client moins élégant. À une époque où il y avait beaucoup plus de boue et de poussière dans les rues des villes, les chaussures exigeaient davantage d'entretien qu'aujourd'hui.

6. Work
Arbeit
Le travail

It was the last great age of coal. Coal powered factories,
ships and railways, gave up its gas for fires and lighting,
and drove the turbines and generators producing electricity.
French miners, deep underground, 1909.

Das letzte große Zeitalter der Kohle. Mit Kohle wurden
Fabriken, Schiffe und Eisenbahnen betrieben, Kohle spendete
Energie für Öfen und Beleuchtung und trieb Turbinen sowie
Generatoren zur Erzeugung von Elektrizität an. Französische
Grubenarbeiter unter Tage, 1909.

C'était la grande époque du charbon. Le charbon faisait
tourner les usines et avancer les bateaux et les trains,
alimentait les poêles et les réverbères, mais aussi les turbines
et les générateurs d'électricité. Des mineurs français au fond
du trou, 1909.

6. Work
Arbeit
Le travail

It was not an age that believed in the wisdom of keeping a percentage of the workforce idle. At daybreak, across the world, people trudged through the gates of factories, collieries, foundries; through the doors of offices, shops and stores; into fields, forests and pastures.

When times were bad, they were locked out and gathered in groups small and large on the docksides, on street corners or at the factory gates – begging, praying and sometimes battling for work. Economic depression was not unknown, but it had yet to reach the acute and chronic levels that were to come later in the century. It was just as well. Few governments had much to offer by way of social security.

Others lived where they worked. Hundreds of thousands of men and women spent their lives in domestic service, as butlers, valets, cooks, gardeners, maids, footmen, coachmen and – increasingly – chauffeurs. Millions more worked at home – in the sweatshops of London, Berlin, Paris, New York, Madrid, St Petersburg and a thousand more cities; in dimly-lit rooms where they stitched and sewed; around tables where they assembled toys and cheap jewellery; and in their tiny gardens where they cut flowers and picked vegetables.

There was work for all – but fortune for so few.

In diesem Zeitalter war es unklug, Arbeitskräfte unbeschäftigt zu lassen. Bei Tagesanbruch trotteten überall auf der Welt Menschen durch die Tore von Fabriken, Zechen, Gießereien, durch die Türen von Büros, Läden und Kaufhäusern, auf Felder und in Wald und Flur.

In schlechten Zeiten wurden sie ausgesperrt. Dann sammelten sie sich in kleinen und großen Gruppen in den Häfen, an Straßenecken oder an den Fabriktoren und baten, bettelten und kämpften manchmal sogar um Arbeit. Wirtschaftskrisen waren nicht unbekannt, doch die Wirtschaft sollte ihren brisanten und lang andauernden Tiefstand erst später in diesem Jahrhundert erreichen. Das war vielleicht gut so. Viele Regierungen hatten kaum etwas im Hinblick auf soziale Sicherheit zu bieten.

Andere lebten dort, wo sie arbeiteten. Hunderttausende Männer und Frauen verbrachten ihr Leben als Hausangestellte, Butler, Kammerdiener, Köche, Gärtner, Hausmädchen, Lakaien, Kutscher und zunehmend als Chauffeure. Millionen von Menschen arbeiteten in den Ausbeuterbetrieben in London, Berlin, Paris, New York, Madrid, St. Petersburg und in tausend anderen Städten. Sie arbeiteten in schlecht beleuchteten Räumen, in denen sie stickten und nähten, saßen dicht gedrängt an Tischen und setzten Spielzeug und billigen Schmuck zusammen. In ihren Gärten schnitten sie Blumen oder ernteten Gemüse.

Arbeit gab es für alle, doch Wohlstand nur für sehr wenige.

C'était une époque à laquelle l'on n'envisageait pas de laisser oisive une seule fraction des forces de travail. Dès l'aube, un peu partout dans le monde, les hommes se pressaient aux portes des usines, des mines de charbon, des fonderies ; dans les bureaux, les boutiques et les grands magasins ; dans les champs, dans les forêts et sur les pâturages.

Quand les temps étaient durs, ils étaient licenciés et se réunissaient aux coins des rues ou aux portes des usines, priant et parfois bataillant pour obtenir du travail. La dépression économique n'était pas inconnue, mais elle n'avait pas encore atteint les niveaux aigus et chroniques qui devaient marquer des périodes plus tardives dans le siècle. C'était bien, car peu de gouvernements avaient beaucoup à offrir en termes de sécurité sociale.

Certains vivaient là où ils travaillaient. Des milliers d'hommes et de femmes passaient leurs vies à servir les autres : majordomes, valets de chambre, valets de pieds, cuisiniers, jardiniers, femmes de chambre, cochers et, bientôt, chauffeurs. En outre des millions de gens travaillaient là où ils vivaient : dans les ateliers clandestins de Londres, Berlin, Paris, New York, Madrid, Saint-Pétersbourg et dans mille autres villes ; dans des chambres mal éclairées où ils piquaient et cousaient ; autour de tables où ils assemblaient des jouets et des bijoux de fantaisie ; dans leurs minuscules jardins où ils faisaient pousser des fleurs et des légumes.

Il y avait du travail pour tous, mais de la fortune pour très peu d'entre eux.

The cats and dogs meat man with some of his non-paying customers in a London street, 1900. The supervision of Public Health had improved to the point where at least some meat was declared unfit for human consumption.

Der Katzen- und Hundefutterverkäufer mit einigen seiner nicht zahlenden Kunden auf einer Londoner Straße, 1900. Aufgrund der verbesserten Kontrollen seitens der Gesundheitsbehörden wurde zumindest ein Teil des Fleisches als ungeeignet für den menschlichen Verzehr erklärt.

Le vendeur de viande pour chats et pour chiens, face à quelques uns de ses clients « non-payants », dans une rue de Londres, 1900. Le contrôle de la Santé publique s'était amélioré et avait même décrété certaines viandes impropres à la consommation humaine.

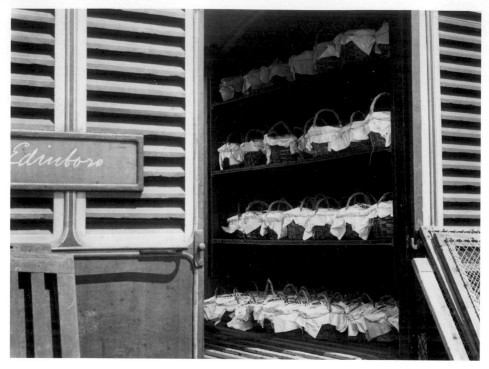

Fruit from Hampshire awaits despatch to Edinburgh, 1902. Fruit and
vegetables were only available 'in season' at the beginning of the 20th century.
The strawberry season was a short one – a few weeks in June and July.

Obst aus Hampshire liegt für den Versand nach Edinburgh bereit, 1902.
Zu Beginn des 20. Jahrhunderts war Obst und Gemüse nur in der jeweiligen
Saison erhältlich. Die Erdbeersaison war sehr kurz, sie dauerte nur einige
Wochen im Juni und Juli.

Dans le Hampshire, des fruits attendent d'être envoyés à Édimbourg, 1902.
Au début du XXᵉ siècle, on ne trouvait bien sûr que des fruits et des légumes
de saison. La saison des fraises était très courte, quelques semaines à peine en
juin et juillet.

A family of strawberry pickers enjoys a break from work in a Hampshire field, 1902. They were almost certainly local people. At other times of year there would be potatoes to dig, or watercress to pick. Much of the time, there would be no work at all.

Eine Erdbeerpflückerfamilie bei einer Arbeitspause in einem Feld bei Hampshire, 1902. Wahrscheinlich waren dort nur Ortsansässige beschäftigt. In anderen Jahreszeiten mussten Kartoffeln geerntet oder Brunnenkresse gepflückt werden. Doch die meiste Zeit gab es überhaupt keine Arbeit.

Une famille de cueilleurs de fraises pendant la pause, dans un champs du Hampshire, 1902. C'étaient presque certainement des gens de la région. À d'autres périodes de l'année, ils déterraient les pommes de terre ou ramassaient le cresson. La plupart du temps, ils n'avaient pas de travail du tout.

Grinding out a living on the city streets. (Opposite) Eugène Atget's albumen portrait of a knife grinder in Paris, c. 1900. (Above) Paul Martin's photograph of children gathered round a street organ, complete with monkeys, c. 1900.

Man verdiente sich seinen Lebensunterhalt auf der Straße. (Gegenüberliegende Seite) Eugène Atgets Albuminporträt eines Scherenschleifers in Paris, um 1900. (Oben) Paul Martins Aufnahme zeigt eine um eine große Straßenorgel versammelte Menge von Kindern, auch die Äffchen fehlen dabei nicht, um 1900.

Gagner son pain, qu'il vente ou qu'il pleuve. (Ci-contre) Le portrait à l'albumine, par Eugène Atget, d'un rémouleur parisien, vers 1900. (Ci-dessus) Photo de Paul Martin : des enfants assemblés autour d'un orgue de barbarie avec des singes, vers 1900.

Although laws had been passed preventing children from digging coal, there was still plenty for young lads in mines and collieries. (Opposite) Cleaning coal in Bargoed, South Wales. (Above) Unloading coal barges in St Petersburg, Russia, 1900.

Obwohl Kinderarbeit beim Kohleabbau gesetzlich verboten war, gab es viele junge Burschen in den Bergwerken und Zechen. (Gegenüberliegende Seite) Die Kohle wird in Bargoed, South Wales, gesäubert. (Oben) In St. Petersburg werden Kohleschlepp-kähne entladen, Russland, 1900.

En dépit d'une loi qui interdisait d'employer des enfants dans les mines de charbon, on trouvait encore beaucoup de jeunes garçons dans les mines et les houillères. (Ci-contre) Le nettoyage du charbon à Bargoed, au sud du Pays de Galles. (Ci-dessus) Extraction du charbon dans des brouettes à Saint-Pétersbourg, Russie, 1900.

Miners arrive at the foot of the shaft to begin their shift, 1900. They needed to get there speedily: they would be paid from the time they reached the coalface.

Bergarbeiter kommen zum Schichtbeginn unten im Schacht an, 1900. Das musste schnell gehen, denn erst dann wurden sie bezahlt.

Des mineurs arrivent au pied du puits pour prendre leur poste, 1900. Ils leur fallait se dépêcher, car ils n'étaient payés qu'à partir du moment où ils atteignaient le front de taille.

Some ten hours later, miners wait to go back to the surface at the end of their shift, Bargoed, South Wales. Young boys often helped shunt the coal wagons along the rails, or worked with the pit ponies.

Ungefähr 10 Stunden später warten die Bergarbeiter bei Schichtende auf ihre Rückkehr nach oben, Bargoed, South Wales. Junge Burschen halfen oft beim Rangieren der Kohleloren auf den Schienen, oder sie arbeiteten mit den Grubenponys.

Quelques dix heures plus tard, après leur travail, les mineurs attendent de remonter à la surface, Bargoed, Galles du Sud. Souvent, de jeunes garçons aidaient à l'aiguillage des wagonnets ou faisaient travailler les poneys de mines.

Sacks of hops await collection from a Hampshire farm, 1902. In France, Germany,
Belgium, Britain and the United States, beer was the working man's drink. It slaked his
thirst and drowned some of his sorrows.

Hopfensäcke stehen für die Abholung auf einer Farm in Hampshire bereit, 1902.
In Frankreich, Deutschland, Belgien, Großbritannien und in den Vereinigten Staaten war
Bier das Getränk der Arbeiter. Es löschte den Durst und ertränkte so manche Sorgen.

Des sacs de houblon attendent d'être emportés de cette ferme du Hampshire, 1902.
En France, en Allemagne, en Belgique, en Grande-Bretagne et aux États-Unis, la bière
était la boisson de l'ouvrier. Elle étanchait sa soif et noyait un peu ses soucis.

More casual work for the country labourer – packing hops at harvest time, 1902.
This is one of many photographs by F J Mortimer, who recorded Hampshire life in the
early 20th century.

Noch mehr Gelegenheitsarbeit für die Arbeiter auf dem Land – zur Erntezeit wird der
Hopfen in Säcke abgefüllt, 1902. Dies ist eine von vielen Fotoaufnahmen von F. J. Mortimer,
der das Leben in Hampshire zu Beginn des 20. Jahrhunderts dokumentierte.

Un travail saisonnier pour les ouvriers agricoles : la mise en balles du houblon au moment
de la récolte. Ceci est l'une des nombreuses photographies réalisées par F. J. Mortimer, qui
consigna les traces de la vie quotidienne dans le Hampshire au début du XXᵉ siècle.

Hastening the harvest. Vegetables are forced under glass domes on a farm, 1908. There were always choice and expensive early crops for the rich in the cities or on local estates. Others had to wait a few weeks longer.

Beschleunigung der Reifezeit. Auf einer Farm wird Gemüse unter kleinen Glaskuppeln gezogen, 1908. Es gab immer eine erstklassige, aber auch teure Frühernte für die Reichen in den Städten oder auf den Landsitzen vor Ort. Die anderen mussten ein paar Wochen länger warten.

Hâter la récolte. La pousse est accélérée sous ces dômes de verre dans une ferme, 1908. Il y a toujours eu moyen d'offrir aux riches des villes ou des propriétés de campagne de la variété et de la précocité. Les autres devaient se contenter d'attendre quelques semaines de plus.

Preserving the vintage. Thousands of bottles of champagne bide their time in the cellars at Reims, France, that have existed since Roman times. Here the tiny bubbles formed that would later delight and intoxicate their consumers.

Lagerung der Weinernte. Tausende von Champagnerflaschen warten auf ihren Augenblick der vollen Reife in den Weinkellern von Reims, Frankreich. Diese Weinkeller gibt es dort bereits seit der Römerzeit. Hier entstehen die kleinen Bläschen, die später die Kunden erfreuen und berauschen sollen.

Soigner la récolte. Des milliers de bouteilles de champagne attendent leur heure dans des caves qui existent depuis l'époque romaine, à Reims. C'est ici que se forment les petites bulles qui raviront et griseront les amateurs.

A stockier version
of Eliza Doolittle.
One of London's
many flower sellers,
Regent Street, 1900.

Eine stämmigere
Ausführung von
Eliza Doolittle. Eine
der vielen Blumen-
verkäuferinnen in
London, Regent
Street, 1900.

Une Eliza Doolittle
plus en chair. L'une
des nombreuses
fleuristes de Londres,
Regent Street, 1900.

Not long out of school, but already earning a living, a boy refreshes
himself with a glass of sherbet water, Cheapside, London, 1900.
It would have cost him a ha'penny – roughly a fifth of a modern pence.

Dieser Junge ist noch nicht lange mit der Schule fertig, verdient
aber schon seinen Lebensunterhalt. Hier erfrischt er sich mit einem
Glas Brausewasser, Cheapside, London, 1900. Diese hatte ihn wohl
einen halben Penny gekostet – ungefähr ein Fünftel eines heutigen
Pence-Stücks.

Ce garçon, écolier il y a peu encore, gagne déjà sa vie et se rafraîchit
ici d'un verre de limonade, Cheapside, Londres, 1900. Il lui en coûtait
un demi penny, environ 20 centimes d'aujourd'hui.

Chefs prepare for a busy shift in the kitchens of the Hotel Cecil in London's West End, 1900. The Cecil was a famous hotel where the rich and famous, discerning and demanding, stayed.

Köche bereiten sich auf eine arbeitsreiche Schicht in der Großküche des Hotels Cecil im Londoner West End vor, 1900. Das Cecil war ein ausgezeichnetes Hotel, in dem die Reichen und Berühmten, die Gebildeten und Anspruchsvollen logierten.

Des chefs se préparent à un service chargé dans les cuisines de l'Hôtel Cecil dans le West End de Londres, 1900. Le Cecil était un hôtel célèbre, fréquenté par une élite raffinée et exigeante.

Women packers in a factory that produced syrups and bottled fruit, 1900. Although a greater variety of jobs was available for women, most were still employed as domestic servants.

Packerinnen in einer Fabrik, in der Sirup hergestellt und Obst eingemacht wurde, 1900. Obwohl es eine größere Vielfalt an Tätigkeiten für Frauen gab, waren die meisten von ihnen immer noch als Hausangestellte beschäftigt.

Des femmes chargées du conditionnement dans une usine de production de sirops et de fruits en bouteilles, 1900. Bien qu'une assez grande diversité d'emplois s'offrît aux femmes, la plupart travaillaient encore comme domestiques.

Early NYPD Blues. Members of the
New York City Police Department
with their sergeant parade in uniform
before going out on patrol, c. 1900.
Their helmets appear to be in a
transitional stage between those
of the British and the modern
American policeman.

Trübsinnige Stimmung am Morgen
im New York City Police Department
(NYPD). Mitglieder des Departments
in Uniform bei ihrer Parade, bevor sie
auf Streife gehen, um 1900. Bei ihren
Helmen handelt es sich scheinbar um
eine Übergangslösung zwischen denen
der britischen und denen der heutigen
amerikanischen Polizei.

NYPD blues, version ancienne.
Des membres du New York City
Police Department avec leur sergent
se présentent en uniforme et en
rangs avant de sortir en patrouilles,
vers 1900. Leurs casques semblent
figurer une sorte de transition entre
ceux de la police britannique et ceux
du policier américain actuel.

A team of firemen, somewhere in England, direct their hose at a fire inside a building, 1909. Fire was an everyday hazard in the days of open hearths, draughts and a wealth of combustible material.

Drei Feuerwehrmänner irgendwo in England beim Löschen eines Brands, 1909. Feuer war eine alltägliche Gefahr in Zeiten von offenen Feuerstellen, Durchzug und reichlich brennbarem Material.

Quelque part en Angleterre, une équipe de pompiers dirige sa lance sur un incendie à l'intérieur d'un immeuble, 1909. À cette époque où les foyers étaient ouverts à tous les vents et où les matériaux combustibles ne manquaient pas, chaque jour voyait son lot d'incendies.

A team of horses, somewhere
in the United States, provide
the motive power for a
steam-driven fire appliance.
It must have been a fearsome
sight – more frightening
than the fire itself.

Drei Pferde ziehen irgendwo
in den Vereinigten Staaten
einen mit Dampf ange-
triebenen Feuerwehrwagen.
Es muss ein Furcht erregender
Anblick gewesen sein –
beängstigender als das
Feuer selbst.

Quelque part aux États-Unis,
un attelage de chevaux
fournit la force motrice de
cette autopompe à vapeur.
La vision de cet équipage
produisait encore plus
d'effroi que l'incendie
lui-même.

Fire! in America, 1900

Russian convicts at work on the eastern section of the Trans-Siberian railway, 1900. It was completed in 1902, though it took another three years of inspection, protection and organisation before it opened.

Russische Sträflinge bei der Arbeit am östlichen Abschnitt der Transsibirischen Eisenbahn, 1900. Fertig gestellt wurde sie im Jahre 1902, obwohl Prüfung, Bewachung und Organisation bis zu ihrer Einweihung weitere drei Jahre in Anspruch nahmen.

Des prisonniers russes travaillant sur la section orientale du chemin de fer transsibérien, 1900. Le parcours fut achevé en 1902, même s'il fallut encore un an de vérifications, de renforcement des protections et d'efforts d'organisation avant de pouvoir ouvrir la ligne.

Women operatives at their looms in the winding room of a Lancashire
cotton mill. The hours were long, the work was hard, but in good times
the money they earned raised the entire family's standard of living.

Arbeiterinnen an ihren Webstühlen im Spulenraum einer Baumwoll-
spinnerei in Lancashire. Es war ein langer und harter Arbeitstag, doch in
guten Zeiten konnten sie mit dem verdienten Geld den Lebensstandard
ihrer Familie anheben.

Des ouvrières à leur métier dans la salle de bobinage d'une cotonnerie
du Lancashire. Les journées étaient longues et le travail était dur, mais en
période faste, l'argent qu'elles gagnaient pouvait élever le niveau de vie
de toute leur famille.

Black cotton pickers in the American South, 1900. Though slavery had been abolished, the pay barely kept body and soul together.

Schwarze Baumwoll-pflücker im amerikanischen Süden, 1900. Obwohl die Sklaverei abgeschafft worden war, konnten sie mit dem Lohn kaum das Essen bezahlen, um Leib und Seele zusammenzuhalten.

Des cueilleurs de coton noir dans le sud des États-Unis, 1900. L'esclavage avait été aboli, mais la paie suffisait à peine à faire vivre un homme.

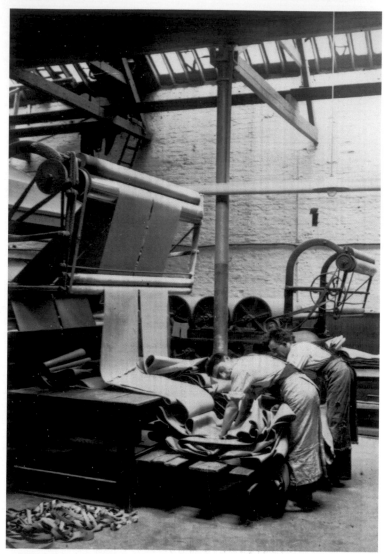

Workers folding and starching linen in a Belfast factory at the turn of the century. The production of linen was a staple industry of Northern Ireland.

Arbeiter beim Falten und Stärken von Leinen in einer Fabrik in Belfast um die Jahrhundertwende. Die Leinenproduktion war ein Hauptindustriezweig in Nordirland.

Des ouvriers pliant et amidonnant des draps de lin dans une usine de Belfast, au tournant du siècle. La production du lin était une industrie importante dans le nord de l'Irlande.

On the other side of the Atlantic a group of tailors – probably from the same immigrant family – ply their trade in a New York tenement, 1900. Few worked longer hours than these contract workers.

Auf der anderen Seite des Atlantiks geht eine Gruppe von Schneidern – wahrscheinlich Einwanderer einer einzigen Familie – ihrer Arbeit in einem New Yorker Mietshaus nach, 1900. Nur wenige arbeiteten länger als diese Auftragsarbeiter.

De l'autre côté de l'Atlantique, un groupe de tailleurs – probablement tous issus de la même famille d'émigrés – s'active dans un taudis de New York, 1900. Peu de gens travaillaient plus d'heures que ces travailleurs à forfait.

Dockers unload barrels from a ship in Portsmouth harbour, on the
English south coast, 1900. British dockers were among the most
militant in the early 20th century, and among the most poorly paid.

Hafenarbeiter entladen Fässer von einem Schiff im Hafen von
Portsmouth an der englischen Südküste, 1900. Britische Hafenarbeiter
gehörten zu Beginn des 20. Jahrhunderts zu den größten Aufrührern,
und auch zu den am schlechtesten bezahlten.

Des dockers déchargent des barils d'un navire dans le port de
Portsmouth, sur la côte anglaise méridionale, 1900. Les dockers
britanniques étaient parmi les plus militants au début du XXᵉ siècle,
et aussi parmi les plus mal payés.

Lumber is prepared
for use in paper
making, Washington
State, USA, 1900.
It was the state's most
valuable commodity.

Hier wird Holz für die
Papierherstellung vor-
bereitet, Washington,
USA, 1900. Holz
war das wertvollste
Erzeugnis in diesem
Bundesstaat.

Le bois est préparé
pour être transformé
en papier, État de
Washington, USA,
1900. C'était la
matière première
la plus précieuse de
cet État.

The interior of a box tower at a petrol works in Prededussport,
Romania, 1909. More valuable, more sought-after and of
greater use than gold, oil was already beginning to replace coal
in the 1900s.

Das Innere eines Ölförderturms in Prededussport, Rumänien, 1909.
Wertvoller, begehrter und nützlicher noch als Gold begann Öl
bereits mit Beginn des 20. Jahrhunderts die Kohle zu verdrängen.

L'intérieur d'une tour d'extraction sur un puits de pétrole à
Prededussport, Roumanie, 1909. Plus précieux, plus recherché
et plus utile que l'or, le pétrole commençait déjà à remplacer le
charbon dans les années 1900.

An oilfield at Saratoga, Texas, April 1908. The biggest oil producer in the world was the United States, and the heart of the American oil industry was in Texas.

Ein Ölfeld in Saratoga, Texas, April 1908. Der weltweit größte Ölförderer waren die Vereinigten Staaten. Das Herz der amerikanischen Ölindustrie lag in Texas.

Un champ de pétrole à Saratoga, Texas, avril 1908. Les États-Unis étaient le plus grand producteur de pétrole au monde et le cœur de l'industrie pétrolière américaine était au Texas.

(Above) The wild days of the American West were over, but there was still plenty of work for ranch hands at the Matador Ranch, Texas, 1908, photographed by Erwin E Smith. (Opposite) Itinerant sheep shearers, Westmoreland, England, 1900.

(Oben) Die wilden Tage des amerikanischen Westens waren gezählt. Doch gab es immer noch reichlich Arbeit für Farmhelfer auf der Matador Ranch, Texas, 1908, aufgenommen von Erwin E. Smith. (Gegenüberliegende Seite) Wanderschafscherer, Westmoreland, England, 1900.

(Ci-dessus) La grande époque de l'Ouest américain était passée, mais il y avait encore largement de quoi s'occuper au Matador Ranch, Texas, 1908 ; photographie d'Erwin E. Smith. (Ci-contre) Tondeurs de mouton itinérants, Westmoreland, Angleterre, 1900.

In an age that was only just beginning to flirt with impropriety, there was still employment for this bathing-machine attendant, somewhere on the coast of England, 1900. But a new morality threatened.

In einer Zeit, in der man gerade erst mit dem Gedanken der Unschicklichkeit zu spielen begann, gab es immer noch Arbeit für diese Wärterin mobiler Umkleidekabinen, irgendwo an der Küste Englands, 1900. Neue Moralvorstellungen waren jedoch im Kommen.

À une époque qui commençait tout juste à s'adonner à l'inconvenance, il y avait encore du travail pour cette gardienne de cabines de bain mobiles, quelque part sur la côte anglaise, 1900. Mais une nouvelle morale était sur le point de voir le jour.

New Year's Day 1909, and a new Act comes into force: some 500,000 elderly in Britain – including these two – become pensioners for the first time, eligible for weekly payments from the Government.

Neujahrstag 1909. Ein neues Gesetz tritt in Kraft. Ungefähr 500 000 ältere Menschen in Groß-britannien – wie diese beiden hier – erhalten zum ersten Mal Rente. Sie haben Anspruch auf wöchentliche Zahlungen von der Regierung.

Le jour du Nouvel An 1909, une nouvelle loi entre en application : en Grande-Bretagne, quelques 500 000 personnes âgées (dont les deux que l'on voit ici) se voyaient ouvrir le droit à une pension de retraite que le gouvernement leur versait chaque semaine.

7. Leisure
Freizeit
Les loisirs

It was the simplest, happiest and most innocent of pleasures.
A day at the seaside meant donkey rides and ice-creams, walks along
the esplanade, fun at the slot machines, and paddling in the sea.
Two women enjoy the delights of the beach, 1902.

Das einfachste, amüsanteste und harmloseste Freizeitvergnügen.
Ein Tag am Meer mit Eselsritten, Eis, Spaziergängen auf der Strand-
promenade, Spaß an Spielautomaten und Badevergnügen im Meer.
Zwei Frauen amüsieren sich ausgelassen am Strand, 1902.

C'était le plus simple, le plus heureux et le plus innocent des plaisirs.
Un jour à la mer signifiait promenades à dos d'âne et crèmes glacées,
déambulations sur l'esplanade, amusement aux machines à sous,
ballades à la rame sur l'eau. Deux femmes font l'expérience des
délices du bain de mer, 1902.

7. Leisure
Freizeit
Les loisirs

Wages were rising early in the 20th century, and the pioneer work of Thomas Cook and his 'day excursions' a generation earlier was greatly extended by the rapid development of the internal combustion engine. Nowhere was safe from the whirring wheels of the tripper, the tourist, the excursionist. Families and courting couples, historical societies and Sunday schools, young 'blades' in boaters and young 'gels' in fancy hats, all flocked to the country-side, the moors, the woods and, above all, the seaside.

Leisure was an active experience for the Edwardians and their contemporaries. The public baths, the public libraries, many of the pubs and almost all other institutions were closed on Sundays. There remained the great outdoors, and that is where many went.

But the seaside was always the favourite destination. Brighton, Atlantic City, Coney Island, Le Touquet, Deauville, San Sebastian, Nice and Monte-Carlo (for those who could afford it) grew in size and wealth and in the number of joys that they had to offer. There were piers and Pierrots, aquariums and amusement arcades, brass bands and bathing machines, saucy delights and mile after mile of golden sand. For a while at least, the desk, the loom, the coalface and the school desk seemed a lifetime away.

Die zu Beginn des 20. Jahrhunderts ansteigenden Löhne sowie die rasche Fortentwicklung des Verbrennungsmotors ließen die von Thomas Cook ins Leben gerufenen „Tagesausflüge" mehr und mehr in Mode kommen. Nichts war sicher vor den ratternden Rädern der Ausflügler, Urlauber und Feriengäste. Familien und Pärchen, historische Gesellschaften und Sonntagsschulen, junge Männer mit Strohhüten oder junge Mädchen mit ausgefallenen Hüten, sie alle strömten in Scharen aufs Land, in die Moorlandschaften, die Wälder und vor allem ans Meer.

Für die Zeitgenossen Edwards VII. war Freizeit eine neue Erfahrung. Sonntags waren die öffentlichen Bäder, Bibliotheken, viele Lokale und fast alle anderen Einrichtungen geschlossen. Da blieb einem nur die freie Natur und dorthin begab man sich dann auch.

Das Meer war und blieb jedoch das beliebteste Ausflugsziel. Brighton, Atlantic City, Coney Island, Le Touquet, Deauville, San Sebastian, Nizza und Monte Carlo (für diejenigen, die es sich leisten konnten) wurden größer, der Reichtum nahm zu, und die angebotenen Freizeitmöglichkeiten wurden zahlreicher. Dort gab es Piere und Pierrots, Aquarien und Amüsementhallen, Blaskapellen und mobile Umkleidekabinen, ausgefallene Vergnügungsmöglichkeiten und weißen Sandstrand, so weit das Auge reichte. Für eine Weile schien der Bürotisch, der Webstuhl, die Zeche oder das Schülerpult in weite Ferne gerückt zu sein.

Au début du XXᵉ siècle, tandis que les salaires augmentaient, l'œuvre pionnière de Thomas Cook et ses « excursions d'un jour » inaugurées une génération plus tôt rencontrèrent un succès croissant grâce au développement du moteur à combustion interne. Aucun lieu n'échappait plus aux roues vrombissantes du vacancier, du touriste ou de l'excursionniste. Les familles, les couples d'amoureux, les sociétés historiques et les écoles du dimanche, les « p'tits gars » en canotiers et les « jeunes dames » en jolis chapeaux, tous déboulaient en foule à la campagne, sur la lande, dans les bois et surtout au bord de la mer.

Les loisirs furent une expérience très active à l'époque édouardienne, pour les Britanniques comme pour les autres. Les bains publics, les bibliothèques publiques, de nombreux pubs et presque toutes les autres institutions étaient fermés le dimanche. Il restait alors la nature dans toute sa variété et beaucoup s'y rendaient.

Mais le bord de mer restait la destination de prédilection. Brighton, Atlantic City, Coney Island, Le Touquet, Deauville, San Sebastian, Nice et Monte-Carlo (pour ceux qui pouvaient se le permettre) croissaient en dimensions et en nombre de plaisirs offerts. Il y avait la promenade sur la jetée, le théâtre de marionnettes, les aquariums et les luna-parks, les fanfares et les cabines de bains roulantes, les corps qui se découvraient un peu et kilomètres de sable doré. Le bureau, l'atelier, la mine et l'école semblaient alors à des années lumières.

The pleasures of the seaside were shared by all, young and old, sophisticated and naïve, the mighty and the humble. Here members of the Rothschild family shelter from the winds of fortune, c. 1909.

Das Vergnügen am Meer fand bei allen großen Anklang – Jung und Alt, der feinen Gesellschaft und den einfachen Leuten, den „Mächtigen" und den „Schmächtigen". Hier suchen Angehörige der Familie Rothschild Schutz vor den Stürmen des Schicksals, um 1909.

Les plaisirs du bord de mer étaient partagés par tous, jeunes et vieux, naïfs et instruits, humbles et puissants. Ici, des membres de la famille Rothschild, bien à l'abri des revers de fortune, vers 1909.

Bathers still used these monstrous bathing machines to change into their costume for a 'dip in the briny'. And horses still pulled them in and out of the sea for the convenience of the modest. An English resort, c. 1909.

Die Badegäste benutzten immer noch diese monströsen fahrbaren Umkleidekabinen, um sich ihre Badeanzüge anzuziehen und dann kurz einmal in die salzige See zu tauchen. Pferde zogen diese Umkleiden ins und aus dem Meer, damit es für die Sittsamen bequemer war. Ein englischer Badeort, um 1909.

Les baigneurs utilisaient encore ces énormes cabines de bain pour se mettre en costume avant de « sauter dans la belle bleue ». Elles étaient tirées par des chevaux qui les amenaient jusque dans l'eau pour le confort des plus modestes. Une station balnéaire anglaise, vers 1909.

The greatest fun of all was to challenge the incoming tide
with the biggest sandcastle anyone had ever made.
Alfred Hind Robinson's lovely panorama of the beach at
Bamburgh, Northumberland, c. 1909, encapsulates the
essence of the pleasure.

Am meisten Spaß machte es, sich der nahenden Flut mit der
größten Sandburg, die jemals gebaut wurde, entgegenzustellen.
Das wunderschöne Panorama von Alfred Hind Robinson vom
Strand bei Bamburgh, Northumberland, um 1909, fängt die
Stimmung dieses Vergnügens sehr gut ein.

Le plus amusant était bien sûr de défier la marée montante avec
le plus grand château de sable de tous les temps. Ce très beau
panorama de plage à Bamburgh, Northumberland, par Alfred
Hind Robinson, vers 1909, capte l'essence de ce plaisir.

They came in their hundreds, to stroll along the promenade in their smartest clothes, with their parasols cocked against the sun – for a tan was most unfashionable. The seafront at Southsea, Portsmouth, in 1900.

Sie kamen in Scharen, um in ihren besten Kleidern und mit ihren gegen die Sonne gerichteten Schirmen – gebräunte Haut war ganz und gar nicht in Mode – über die Promenade zu flanieren. Die Strandpromenade von Southsea, Portsmouth, im Jahre 1900.

Ils venaient par centaines déambuler le long de la promenade dans leurs plus beaux habits, protégés du soleil par leurs ombrelles – car le bronzage n'était pas encore à la mode. Le front de mer à Southsea, Portsmouth, 1900.

In winter there was no better delight than a sing-song around the piano in the parlour. The repertoire was varied – ballads, novelty songs, arias from light opera. One of the most popular of all was *I Do Like To Be Beside The Seaside*. A family gathering around the piano, 1908.

Im Winter gab es nichts Schöneres, als im Wohnzimmer um das Klavier versammelt ein paar Lieder zu singen. Das Repertoire reichte von Balladen über neuere Lieder bis hin zu Arien aus Operetten. Eine der beliebtesten war *I Do Like To Be Beside The Seaside*. Eine Familie hat sich hier um das Klavier versammelt, 1908.

L'hiver, il n'y avait pas de plaisir plus grand que de se réunir pour chanter autour du piano, dans le salon. Le répertoire était varié : ballades, chansons à la mode, arias d'opérettes. L'un des airs les plus appréciés était *I Do Like To Be Beside The Seaside* (« J'aime tellement les bords de mer »). Une famille autour du piano, 1908.

Good weather was not essential. A lungful of ozone was as beneficial on
a bracing day as on a fine one. Late Victorian ladies gaze at the splendours
of Eastbourne pier on a cold day in 1900.

Gutes Wetter war nicht so wichtig. Ein tiefer Atemzug an der frischen Luft
tat bei schlechtem Wetter genauso gut wie bei gutem. Spätviktorianische
Damen blicken hier an einem kühlen Tag im Jahre 1900 auf den prächtigen
Pier von Eastbourne.

Le beau temps n'était pas indispensable. Une bouffée d'air frais était aussi
bénéfique pour les poumons par vent que par soleil. Des dames de la fin de
l'ère victorienne contemplent les beautés de la jetée d'Eastbourne par un
jour froid de 1900.

Better than gazing at the pier was to saunter along it. You could weigh yourself, have your fortune told, win a prize, buy a stick of rock, meet the boy or girl of your dreams. Holidaymakers on the Clarence Pier, Southsea, 1900.

Noch schöner, als sich den Pier bloß anzusehen, war es, über ihn zu flanieren. Dort konnte man sich wiegen, sich die Zukunft voraussagen lassen, Preise gewinnen, Zuckerstangen kaufen oder das Mädchen oder den Jungen seiner Träume treffen. Urlauber auf dem Clarence Pier, Southsea, 1900.

Il était encore mieux de flâner sur la jetée que de la regarder. On pouvait se peser, se faire dire l'avenir, remporter un prix, acheter un bout de roche ou rencontrer l'homme ou la femme de ses rêves. Des vacanciers sur le Clarence Pier, Southsea, 1900.

The notion of animal rights had not yet cramped the style of visitors to the zoo.
(Above) Young people enjoy an elephant ride in Regent's Park, London, 1900.
(Opposite) A leopard studies an example of the species *Homo sapiens*.

Der Begriff „Tierschutz" hielt die Leute zu dieser Zeit noch nicht von einem
Besuch im Zoo ab. (Oben) Kinder haben Spaß an einem Ritt auf einem Elefanten
im Regent's Park, London, 1900. (Gegenüberliegende Seite) Ein Leopard mustert
aufmerksam ein Exemplar der Spezies *Homo sapiens*.

La notion de droits des animaux n'embarrassait pas encore les visiteurs du zoo.
(Ci-dessus) Un éléphant faisant à des jeunes gens les honneurs de Regent's Park,
Londres, 1900. (Ci-contre) Un léopard étudie un exemplaire de l'espèce *homo sapiens*.

When it comes to Christmas shopping, little has changed in a hundred years.
The notice on the front of this London store begs customers to shop early.
They did not then (c. 1909). They do not now.

Der weihnachtliche Einkaufstrubel hat sich in den vergangenen 100 Jahren
nicht wesentlich verändert. Das kleine Plakat an der Vorderseite dieses Londoner
Kaufhauses ruft die Kunden dazu auf, möglichst frühzeitig ihre Einkäufe zu
tätigen. Sie taten es damals nicht (um 1909) und sie tun es heute nicht.

Pour ce qui est des courses de Noël, les choses ont peu changé en cent ans.
Sur le fronton de ce magasin de Londres, un placard conseille instamment aux
clients de s'y prendre à l'avance. Ce qu'ils ne faisaient pas alors (vers 1909),
ils ne le font pas davantage aujourd'hui.

Crowds gather around the windows of a store in London's Oxford Street, Christmas 1905. It was a good time to be rich enough to buy presents, wait while they were perfectly wrapped, then take them home in a taxi.

Eine Menschenmenge drängt sich vor den Schaufenstern eines Kaufhauses in der Oxford Street in London, Weihnachten 1905. Wohl dem, der zu dieser Zeit reich genug war, um Geschenke einzukaufen. Man wartete, während diese schön verpackt wurden, und brachte die Geschenke dann im Taxi nach Hause.

Les foules s'agglutinent devant les vitrines d'un magasin d'Oxford Street, à Londres, Noël 1905. C'était le moment d'être assez aisé pour acheter des cadeaux, patienter jusqu'à ce qu'ils soient soigneusement empaquetés et repartir en taxi avec son butin.

For many, the great outdoors beckoned. On Sunday (the only
day free from work) you could cycle in a group to the countryside,
or hire a charabanc to take you. And then, there were all the joys
of a picnic.

Viele zog es in die freie Natur. Am Sonntag (dem einzigen arbeits-
freien Tag in der Woche) radelte man mit ein paar Freunden aufs
Land, oder man mietete sich einen Pferdeomnibus. Dann genoss
man ein herrliches Picknick im Freien.

Pour beaucoup, c'était l'appel des espaces verts. Le dimanche
(unique jour de congé), on partait en groupe à la campagne, à
bicyclette ou en carriole. Puis, c'étaient les joies du pique-nique.

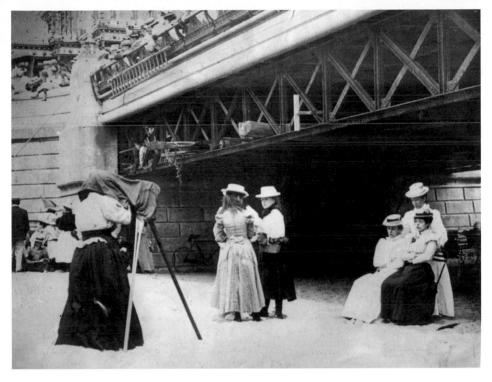

A woman photographer at work on Southend beach, June 1905. For Londoners, the two most popular seaside destinations were Brighton and Southend. Brighton was bigger and brasher, but Southend had the world's longest pier.

Eine Fotografin bei der Arbeit am Strand von Southend, Juni 1905. Brighton und Southend waren für die Londoner die beliebtesten Ausflugsziele am Meer. Brighton war groß und bunt, doch Southend hatte den längsten Pier der Welt.

Une femme photographe à l'œuvre sur la plage de Southend, juin 1905. Pour les habitants de Londres, Brighton et Southend étaient les destinations balnéaires les plus en vogue. Brighton était plus grande et plus animée, mais Southend possédait la plus longue jetée du monde.

For the more adventurous, there were the joys and perils of mountaineering.
Clothes were hardly designed for the rigours of the descent into a crevasse
on the Mer de Glace, but they may well have softened the landing in the event
of a fall.

Wer abenteuerlustiger war, der suchte sein Vergnügen, aber auch die Gefahr
beim Bergsteigen. Es gab kaum Kleidung, die für die raue Witterung bei einem
Abstieg in eine Gletscherspalte des Mer de Glace geeignet war, doch im Falle
eines Falles war man gut gepolstert.

Pour les plus aventureux, il y avait les joies et les dangers de la montagne.
Les vêtements étaient rarement appropriés aux rigueurs d'une descente dans une
crevasse de la mer de Glace, mais ils pouvaient éventuellement amortir une chute.

Rock climbing
was for the truly
athletic – and for
those who could
never imagine a
rope fraying on
a rock edge.

Klettern an Fels-
wänden war etwas
für wahre Athleten –
und auch für die-
jenigen, die sich nicht
vorstellen konnten,
dass sich ein Seil
an einer Felskante
durchscheuert.

La varappe était
réservée aux
véritables athlètes –
et à ceux qui
n'imaginaient même
pas qu'une corde
puisse s'user à
l'arête d'une roche.

Members of the Salvation Army farm colony at Hadleigh, Suffolk, prepare
for the start of a piggy-back race, December 1905. The 'Sally Army' was by
then just over 25 years old and had already done much to relieve poverty.

Mitglieder der Farmkolonie der Heilsarmee bei Hadleigh, Suffolk, sind für
ein Huckepackrennen startbereit, Dezember 1905. Zu diesem Zeitpunkt gab
es die Heilsarmee schon 25 Jahre und sie hatte bereits viel zur Linderung der
Armut beigetragen.

Des membres de la communauté agricole de l'Armée du salut à Hadleigh,
Suffolk, se préparent au départ d'une course à califourchon, décembre 1905.
L'Armée du salut avait à peine 25 ans et avait déjà beaucoup œuvré pour
soulager les effets de la misère.

Early days of health and beauty. A group of women perform gymnastic exercises in the yard of what may well be a training college, 1905. Swedish drill was extremely popular in the 1900s.

Gesundheit und Schönheit zu damaligen Zeiten. Eine Gruppe von Frauen macht Turnübungen im Hof einer wohl zu damaligen Zeiten so genannten pädagogischen Hochschule, 1905. Schwedischer Drill war zu Beginn des 20. Jahrhunderts äußerst beliebt.

Santé et beauté : les débuts. Un groupe de femmes font des exercices d'assouplissement dans la cour de ce qui pourrait bien être une école normale, 1905. La gymnastique suédoise était très à la mode dans les années 1900.

A series of hard
winters in Europe
led to a considerable
increase in the
popularity of
skating. Young
men take to the
ice on a frozen
lake at Courbit
Walsh, Spalding,
Lincolnshire, in
January 1908.

Nach mehreren
kalten Wintern in
Europa, erfreute
sich das Schlitt-
schuhlaufen einer
immer größeren
Beliebtheit. Junge
Burschen auf dem
Eis eines gefrorenen
Sees in Courbit
Walsh, Spalding,
Lincolnshire, im
Januar 1908.

En Europe, une
série d'hivers très
durs produisit un
remarquable regain
d'affection pour
le patin à glace.
Ici, de jeunes gens
s'élancent sur un lac
gelé à Courbit
Walsh, Spalding,
Lincolnshire, en
janvier 1908.

Gentle decline… A young woman takes part in an impromptu
programme of winter sports at Buxton in the English Peak
District, 1904. Her hatpin seems to be withstanding the test.

Sanfte Abfahrt … Eine junge Frau nimmt an einem improvisierten Wintersportprogramm bei Buxton im englischen
Peak District teil, 1904. Ihre Hutnadel scheint diese Prüfung
zu bestehen.

Pente douce … Une jeune femme prend part à un
programme impromptu de sports d'hiver à Buxton dans
le district de Peak, 1904. Son épingle à chapeau semble
bien résister à l'épreuve.

Fast descent... Spectators rise to their feet as an Englishwoman
hurtles past on the Cresta Run at St Moritz, Switzerland, 1908.
Many women wanted considerably more than the vote.

Rasante Abfahrt ... Zuschauer springen auf, als eine Engländerin
auf der Cresta-Rennstrecke bei St. Moritz an ihnen vorbeisaust,
Schweiz, 1908. Viele Frauen wollten weitaus mehr als nur das
Wahlrecht.

Descente rapide ... Des spectateurs sautent sur leurs deux pieds à la
vue de cette Anglaise passant en trombe devant eux sur le parcours
de la course de Cresta à Saint-Moritz, Suisse, 1908. Beaucoup de
femmes voulaient bien davantage que le seul droit de vote.

Hot air balloons
prepare for take-off
from the grounds
of the fashionable
Hurlingham Club,
London, in May
1909.

Heißluftballons kurz
vor dem Start auf
dem Gelände des vor-
nehmen Hurlingham
Clubs, London, im
Mai 1909.

Des montgolfières
sur le point de décol-
ler, sur le terrain du
très chic Hurlingham
Club, Londres, en
mai 1909.

In an age when all true Englishmen believed that Britannia still ruled the waves, the height of the London Season was the Cowes Regatta, held annually off the coast of the Isle of Wight. Britannia was to be severely tested a few years later.

Zur der Zeit, als alle echten Engländer glaubten, dass Großbritannien immer noch die Meere beherrsche, war der Höhepunkt der Londoner Saison die Cowes Regatta, die einmal im Jahr an der Küste der Isle of Wight stattfand. Wenige Jahre später sollte Britannien auf einem harten Prüfstand stehen.

À une époque où pas un Anglais ne doutait de la prépondérance de la Grande-Bretagne sur toutes les mers du globe, le moment culminant de la saison londonienne était la régate de Cowes qui se tenait chaque année au large des côtes de l'île de Wight. Quelques années plus tard, la flotte britannique sera sévèrement éprouvée.

8. Entertainment
Unterhaltung
Divertissements

Mathieson Lang as Philippe Marchiali in the 1909 production
The Prisoner of the Bastille. From its very beginnings, the 'picture palace'
swept all before it. Huge audiences flocked to every converted theatre,
hall, pavilion or purpose-built cinema.

Mathieson Lang in der Rolle des Philippe Marchiali in dem Film
The Prisoner of the Bastille im Jahre 1909. Von Anfang an übertraf das
Lichtspielhaus alles bisher Dagewesene. Zuschauermassen strömten
in jedes umgebaute Theater, jede Halle, jeden Saal und jedes zu diesem
Zweck gebaute Kino.

Mathieson Lang joue Philippe Marchiali dans la production anglaise
du *Prisonnier de la Bastille*, en 1909. Dès le début, le cinématographe
emporta tout sur son passage. Des foules immenses accouraient dans les
théâtres transformés, les salles improvisées, les pavillons convertis ou
les palaces construits pour le cinéma.

8. Entertainment
Unterhaltung
Divertissements

By the mid-1900s 'biographs', 'kinemas' and 'picture palaces' had opened in most towns of any size in Europe and the United States. They were popular and successful beyond the wildest dreams of Georges Méliès – whose dreams tended to be on the wild side. From this time the days of the music-hall and the vaudeville theatre were numbered, though both had many more years of popularity and hilarity ahead of them.

A new invention called the gramophone was beginning to bring the voices and the artistry of the world's top singers and comedians into the parlours of the middle classes. Unlike the cinema, it posed no threat to live performances. More people stepped out onto the dance floors of hotels and assembly rooms, parochial halls and country clubs than ever before. Daringly they danced the tango and the waltz, slipping breathlessly back into their seats for a cup of tea or a refreshing cordial.

As for the entertainers, they no longer performed for predominantly local audiences. Their fame travelled swiftly before them, and they were booked to appear in other cities, states, countries and even other continents. The age of the international star was under way.

Um 1905 hatten „Biographs" (Kinos der ersten Filmproduktionsfirmen in Amerika), Lichtspielhäuser und Filmtheater in fast allen Städten Europas und der Vereinigten Staaten ihre Pforten geöffnet. Sie waren beliebter und erfolgreicher als Georges Méliès es sich in seinen kühnsten Träumen vorgestellt hatte – und seine Träume waren in der Tat von der kühnen Sorte. Von dieser Zeit an waren die großen Tage der Varietés und Revuen gezählt, wenngleich ihnen noch viele Jahre großer Popularität bevorstehen sollten.

Die Erfindung des Grammophons brachte nun die Stimmen und das Können der weltbesten Sänger und Komödianten in die Wohnzimmer des Mittelstandes. Im Gegensatz zum Kino stellte das Grammophon keine Bedrohung für Bühnenaufführungen dar. Immer mehr Leute gingen öfter denn je aus, um sich auf den Tanzflächen in Hotels, Vereins-, Gemeindehäusern und Clubs auf dem Lande zu vergnügen. Dort legten sie einen gewagten Tango oder Walzer aufs Parkett, kehrten dann außer Atem zu ihren Plätzen zurück und tranken einen Tee oder einen erfrischenden Fruchtlikör.

Die Unterhalter selbst traten auch nicht mehr nur vor dem örtlichen Publikum auf. Ihr Ruhm eilte ihnen voraus, und man buchte sie für Auftritte in anderen Städten, Bundesstaaten, Ländern und sogar auf anderen Kontinenten. Das Zeitalter des Weltstars hatte begonnen.

Au milieu des années 1900, des «biographes», des «kinémas» ou les «cinépalaces» avaient ouvert dans la plupart des villes en Europe et aux États-Unis. Ils rencontrèrent un succès que même Georges Méliès – dont les rêves ne manquaient pourtant pas d'ampleur – n'avait pas imaginé. Dès cette époque, les jours du music-hall et du vaudeville étaient comptés, même s'il leur restait encore de belles années de rires et de joyeuse popularité devant eux.

Une nouvelle invention, le gramophone, amenait les voix et le talent des chanteurs et des amuseurs les plus célèbres jusque dans les salons de la classe moyenne. À la différence du cinématographe, le gramophone ne menaçait nullement les arts vivants. Par ailleurs, on accourait plus que jamais aux bals et aux réceptions qui avaient lieu dans les hôtels, les salles paroissiales et les country clubs. On dansait impudemment le tango et la valse avant de se glisser vers sa table hors d'haleine, pour une tasse de thé ou un cordial.

Les comiques ne se contentaient plus d'amuser des audiences locales. Leur célébrité voyageait rapidement et ils n'avaient plus qu'à suivre, se produisant devant des salles combles dans des villes, des régions, des pays et même des continents de plus en plus éloignés. L'époque du vedettariat international avait commencé.

Dance of death. Margarete Geertruida Zelle, better known as Mata Hari, performs her notorious 'Dance of the Seven Veils', 1907.

Totentanz. Margaretha Geertruida Zelle, besser bekannt unter dem Namen Mata Hari, führt ihren berühmt-berüchtigten „Dance of the Seven Veils" auf, 1907.

Danse de la mort. Margarete Geertruida Zelle, mieux connue sous le nom de Mata Hari, exécutant sa célèbre « Danse des sept voiles », 1907.

Her coquetry may well have contributed to her conviction as a spy and her execution by firing squad during the First World War.

Ihre kokette Art mag wohl zu ihrer Verurteilung als Spionin und zu ihrer Hinrichtung durch ein Exekutions-kommando während des Ersten Weltkrieges beigetragen haben.

Sa coquetterie a sans doute contribué à la faire condamner comme espionne et à la faire exécuter par un peloton pendant la Première Guerre mondiale.

Early cinematic violence – French-style. The execution scene from a
Georges Méliès film, *L'histoire d'un crime*, made in 1906. So violent
was the scene considered that it was suppressed by the police.

Gewalt im jungen Film – im französischen Stil. Die Hinrichtungsszene
aus dem Film *L'histoire d'un crime* von Georges Méliès von 1906.
Diese Szene wurde als derart brutal angesehen, dass sie von der Polizei
verboten wurde.

Violence cinématographique précoce – « à la française ». Dans
L'histoire d'un crime de Georges Méliès, tourné en 1906, cette scène
d'exécution fut jugée si violente qu'elle fut censurée par la police et
retirée du film.

Early cinematic violence – American-style. The murder scene from Edwin S Potter's *The Great Train Robbery*, 1903. Despite crude sets and acting, its action and narrative pace made it a huge success.

Gewalt im jungen Film – im amerikanischen Stil. Die Mordszene aus dem Film *The Great Train Robbery* von Edwin S. Potter, 1903. Trotz eines primitiven Szenenaufbaus und schlechtem Schauspiel machte die Handlung und das Erzähltempo diesen Film zu einem großen Erfolg.

Violence cinématographique précoce – « à l'américaine ». La scène du meurtre, dans *The Great Train Robbery* d'Edwin S. Potter, 1903. Malgré des décors rudimentaires et un jeu fruste, le récit et l'action de ce film rencontrèrent un immense succès.

(Opposite) Ehrich Weiss, the rabbi's son who became Harry Houdini, 1900. Houdini was the greatest magician and escapologist of his age. (Above) Signor Martino uses his powers to levitate Mlle Nita on stage, 1900.

(Gegenüberliegende Seite) Der Sohn eines Rabbiners, Ehrich Weiss, wurde 1900 unter dem Künstlernamen Harry Houdini bekannt und war der größte Zauberer und Entfesselungskünstler seiner Zeit. (Oben) Signor Martino lässt dank seiner magischen Kräfte Mlle Nita auf der Bühne schweben, 1900.

(Ci-contre) Ehrich Weiss, fils de rabbin devenu Harry Houdini, 1900. Houdini fut le plus grand magicien et prestidigitateur de son temps. (Ci-dessus) Signor Martino utilise ses pouvoirs pour faire léviter Mlle Nita sur la scène, 1900.

An early jazz band, 1900. The costumes are similar to those worn by bands that led mourners through the streets of New Orleans during a funeral. A saxophone quintet, however, was something of a novelty.

Eine der ersten Jazzbands, 1900. Die Kostüme ähneln denen, die Blaskapellen beim Geleit der Trauergäste durch die Straßen von New Orleans während einer Beerdigung trugen. Ein Saxophonquintett war allerdings schon eine Neuheit.

Un des premiers jazz band, 1900. Les costumes sont proches de ceux des orchestres qui conduisaient les processions de deuil dans les rues de la Nouvelle Orléans. Un quintette de saxophones, toutefois, c'était une nouveauté.

The classic 'cakewalk', photographed in Paris on 13 December 1903. Some black performers already preferred European audiences.

Der klassische „Cakewalk", aufgenommen in Paris am 13. Dezember 1903. Einige schwarze Künstler bevorzugten bereits das europäische Publikum.

Un danseur de « cakewalk » photographié à Paris le 13 décembre 1903. Certains artistes noirs préféraient déjà les audiences européennes.

(Opposite) The last performance at the Lambeth music-hall, south London, 1900. (Right) Dan Leno as the Dame in *Jack and the Beanstalk* at the Drury Lane Theatre.

(Gegenüberliegende Seite) Die letzte Aufführung im Lambeth Varictétheater, im Süden von London, 1900. (Rechts) Dan Leno in der Rolle der komischen Alten in *Jack and the Beanstalk* im Drury Lane Theatre.

(Ci-contre) La dernière représentation du music-hall Lambeth, au sud de Londres, 1900. (À droite) Dan Leno jouant la Dame dans *Jack and the Beanstalk,* au Drury Lane Theatre de Londres.

A risqué and ill-contrived tableau of devils and innocents at Le Cirque music-hall, Paris, 1900. It was an immense success.

Ein gewagtes und schlecht durchdachtes Szenenbild mit Teufeln und Unschuldsengeln im Varieté Le Cirque, Paris, 1900. Es war ein Riesenerfolg.

Un tableau risqué et malencontreux, des diables et des innocents au music-hall Le Cirque, à Paris, 1900. Ce fut un grand succès.

Sex and splendour
at the Folies-Bergère,
1909. The costume
was heavy, and to
dance in it would
have courted disaster.

Prachtvolle Erotik
im Folies-Bergère,
1909. Das Kostüm
war sehr schwer,
und darin zu tanzen
hätte wohl zu einem
Unglück geführt.

Le sexe et la
splendeur aux
Folies-Bergère, 1909.
Danser dans ce lourd
costume aurait
signifié friser la
catastrophe à tous
les instants.

Easter surprise. Actresses, musical comedy stars and sisters Phyllis and Zena Dare pose with a giant egg, 1905.

Eine Osterüberraschung. Die beiden Schwestern Phyllis und Zena Dare, Schauspielerinnen und Varietékünstlerinnen, posieren mit einem riesigen Osterei, 1905.

Surprise de Pâques. Les sœurs Phyllis et Zena Dare, actrices et vedettes de comédies musicales, posant avec un œuf géant, 1905.

Eastern delight. A scene from the comic opera *See-See* by Charles Brookfield and Sidney Jones. Following the success of *The Mikado* and *Chu Chin Chow*, the Orient was much in vogue as a setting for stage musicals.

Fröhliche Ostern. Eine Szene aus der komischen Oper *See-See* von Charles Brookfield und Sidney Jones. Nach dem Erfolg von *The Mikado* und *Chu Chin Chow* war eine im orientalischen Stil gestaltete Kulisse für musikalische Bühnenstücke groß in Mode.

Délices de Pâques. Une scène de l'opéra comique *See-See*, de Charles Brookfield et Sidney Jones. À la suite des succès du *Mikado* et de *Chu Chin Chow,* l'Orient était très en vogue dans les comédies musicales de théâtre.

French cheek…
A young Maurice
Chevalier on a
promotional post-
card advertising his
appearance at
the Casino Fontaine,
c. 1909.

Ein französischer
Lausbub … Der
junge Maurice
Chevalier wirbt
auf einer Postkarte
für seinen Auftritt
im Casino Fontaine,
um 1909.

Un culot bien
français … Le jeune
Maurice Chevalier
sur une carte postale
faisant de la publicité
pour sa propre
apparition au
Casino Fontaine,
vers 1909.

French chic… The singer, dancer and actress Jeanne Marie Bourgeois, known to her adoring audiences as Mistinguett, c. 1900.

Französischer Schick … Jeanne Marie Bourgeois, Sängerin, Tänzerin und Schauspielerin, war ihrem begeisterten Publikum unter dem Namen Mistinguett bekannt, um 1900.

Un chic bien français … Jeanne Marie Bourgeois, chanteuse, danseuse et actrice mieux connue et adulée par son public sous le nom de Mistinguett, vers 1900.

Heroes of the Wild West. (Opposite) 'Buffalo Bill' (William Frederick Cody), c. 1900. (Right) Annie Oakley (Phoebe Anne Oakley Moses).

Helden des Wilden Westens. (Gegenüberliegende Seite) „Buffalo Bill" (William Frederick Cody), um 1900. (Rechts) Annie Oakley (Phoebe Anne Oakley Moses).

Des héros de l'Ouest sauvage. (Ci-contre) « Buffalo Bill » (William Frederick Cody), vers 1900. (À droite) Annie Oakley (Phoebe Anne Oakley Moses).

(Above) The stars of Phineas T Barnum's freak show, c. 1905. From left: Laloo (two bodies), Young Herman (vast chest), J K Coffey (human skeleton), James Morris (rubber face) and Jo Jo (dog face). (Opposite) A close-up of Jo Jo.

(Oben) Die Stars des verrückten Monstrositätenkabinetts von Phineas T. Barnum, um 1905. Von links: Laloo (zwei Körper), Young Herman (großer Brustkorb), J. K. Coffey (menschliches Gerippe), James Morris (Gummigesicht) und Jo Jo (Hundegesicht). (Gegenüberliegende Seite) Eine Nahaufnahme von Jo Jo.

(Ci-dessus) Les stars du spectacle de monstres de Phineas T. Barnum, vers 1905. De gauche à droite : Laloo (deux corps), Young Herman (poitrine énorme), J. K. Coffey (squelette humain), James Morris (visage en caoutchouc) et Jo Jo (tête de chien). (Ci-contre) Portrait de Jo Jo.

The genius of Georges Méliès was that he combined popular elements
of stage magic with the technological opportunities created by the
moving picture. (Above and opposite) Méliès' great metamorphosis.

Die Genialität von Georges Méliès bestand darin, dass er herkömmliche
Elemente der Bühnenzauberei mit den technischen Möglichkeiten der
bewegten Bilder verband. (Oben und gegenüberliegende Seite) Die fantastische
Metamorphose von Méliès.

Le génie de Georges Méliès fut de combiner des éléments de
magie théâtrale avec les possibilités techniques du cinématographe.
(Ci-dessus et ci-contre) La grande métamorphose de Méliès.

It was a simple enough trick to turn a sleeping woman into a butterfly
– though getting the butterfly into the air may have been a little tricky –
but audiences loved it, and Méliès made a fortune.

Es war ein ganz einfacher Trick, eine schlafende Frau in einen Schmetterling
zu verwandeln – doch diesen Schmetterling in die Lüfte abheben zu lassen,
wäre wohl doch etwas schwierig gewesen. Das Publikum aber liebte diese
Nummer, und Méliès machte damit ein Vermögen.

Il était assez simple de transformer une femme endormie en papillon
– même s'il eût été difficile de faire s'envoler ce dernier – mais le public
adorait ça et ce tour fit la fortune de Méliès.

9. The Arts
Kunst
Les arts

The brilliant dancer Adolphe Bolm of the Russian Imperial Ballet Company in the title role of the ballet *Prince Igor*, 1909. At this time Bolm was accompanying Anna Pavlova on her first tours.

Der hervorragende Tänzer Adolphe Bolm der Russian Imperial Ballet Company in der Hauptrolle des Ballettstücks *Prince Igor,* 1909. Zu dieser Zeit begleitete Bolm Anna Pawlowa auf ihren ersten Tourneen.

Le brillant danseur Adolphe Bolm, de la compagnie du Ballet impérial russe, dans le rôle titre du ballet *Le prince Igor,* 1909. À cette époque, Bolm accompagnait Anna Pavlova dans ses premières tournées.

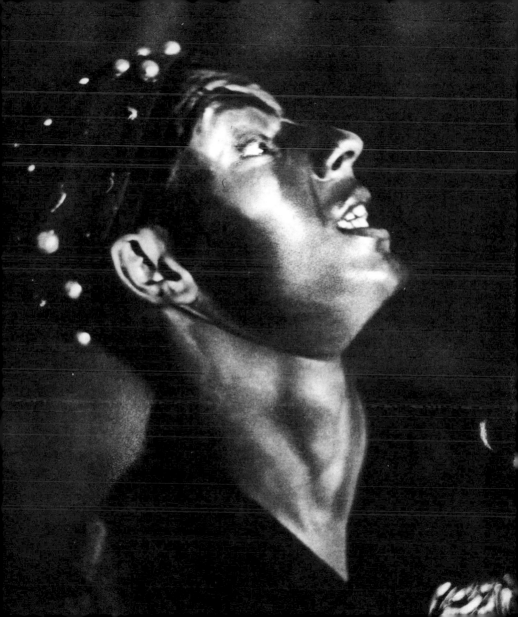

9. The Arts
Kunst
Les arts

Artistically, the 1900s may lay claim to being the most exciting decade the world has ever known. An astonishing array of creative genius poured forth plays and novels, symphonies and scores, poems, sculptures and ideas that transformed the way people viewed the world they lived in. It was the age of Shaw and Strindberg, Braque and Picasso, art nouveau and Auguste Rodin, Schönberg and Mahler, Ravel and de Falla, Elgar and Rachmaninov, E M Forster and H G Wells, the last works of Zola and the first works of Thomas Mann.

The decade began with Freud's *The Interpretation of Dreams* and the first performances of Puccini's *Tosca* and *Madame Butterfly*. It ended with the dancers of Diaghilev's Ballets Russes blazing their way across the stage of the Châtelet in Paris. In 1901 the teenage Picasso set up his studio in Montmartre and painted *The Blue Room*, and the Moscow Art Theatre under Stanislavsky gave the first performance of Chekhov's *Three Sisters*. Every year had its clutch of masterworks, and the audiences flocked to see them.

And then there were the performers, the interpreters… Caruso, Pavlova, Nijinsky, Paderewski, Cortot, Ysaÿe, the young Galli-Curci and the more mature Nellie Melba… Across the Atlantic, Joe 'King' Oliver was beginning to warm up his cornet.

Aus künstlerischer Sicht könnte das erste Jahrzehnt des 20. Jahrhunderts den Anspruch erheben, die aufregendste Dekade zu sein. Eine erstaunliche Anzahl kreativer Talente schuf massenweise Theaterstücke und Romane, Sinfonien und andere Musikstücke, Gedichte, Skulpturen und Ideen, die die Weltanschauung der Menschen veränderten. Es war das Zeitalter von Shaw und Strindberg, Braque und Picasso, von Jugendstil und Auguste Rodin, Schönberg und Mahler, Ravel und de Falla, Elgar und Rachmaninow, E. M. Forster und H. G. Wells, der letzten Werke von Zola und der ersten von Thomas Mann.

Das Jahrzehnt begann mit Freuds *Die Traumdeutung* und der Premiere von Puccinis *Tosca* und *Madame Butterfly*. Es endete mit den Tänzern der Ballets Russes unter Diaghilew, die über die Bühne des Châtelet in Paris wirbelten. Im Jahre 1901 richtete der junge Picasso sein Atelier auf dem Montmartre ein und malte *Das blaue Zimmer*. Die Uraufführung der *Drei Schwestern* von Tschechow wurde vom Moskauer Künstlertheater unter der Leitung von Stanislawski dargeboten. Jedes Jahr brachte neue Meisterwerke hervor und das Publikum strömte herbei, um sie zu sehen.

Und dann waren da noch die Darsteller, die Interpreten ... Caruso, Pawlowa, Nijinskij, Paderewski, Cortot, Ysaÿe, der junge Galli-Curci und die erwachsenere Nellie Melba ... Auf der anderen Seite des Atlantiks fing Joe „King" Oliver an, sein Kornett einzuspielen.

Artistiquement, les années 1900 peuvent briguer la place de décennie la plus prodigieuse de tous les temps. Une stupéfiante palette de talents donna naissance à des romans, des pièces de théâtre, des compositions musicales de tous genres, des poèmes, des sculptures et des idées qui transformèrent entièrement notre manière de voir le monde. Ce fut l'époque de Shaw et de Strindberg, de Braque et de Picasso, de l'Art nouveau et de Rodin, de Schönberg et de Mahler, de Ravel et de de Falla, d'Elgar et de Rachmaninov, d'E. M. Forster et de H. G. Wells, des dernières œuvres de Zola et des premiers écrits de Thomas Mann.

La décennie avait commencé avec *L'interprétation des rêves* de Freud et les premières représentations de *Tosca* et de *Madame Butterfly* de Puccini. Elle s'acheva au moment où les Ballets russes de Diaghilev embrasèrent la scène du Châtelet à Paris. En 1901, Picasso installait son atelier à Montmartre et peignait *La chambre bleue*. Le Théâtre d'art de Moscou, sous la direction de Stanislavski, donnait les premières représentations des *Trois Sœurs* de Tchekhov. Chaque année avait son lot de chefs-d'œuvre et les spectateurs affluaient encore et encore pour les voir.

Et puis il y avait les interprètes, les artistes de la scène ... Caruso, Pavlova, Nijinsky, Paderewski, Cortot, Ysaÿe, Galli-Curci et Nellie Melba dans sa maturité ... Pendant ce temps, de l'autre côté de l'Atlantique, Joe « King » Oliver commençait à chauffer son cornet.

The *corps de ballet*
of the New York
Metropolitan Opera
house take a break
in their Broadway
rehearsal rooms,
September 1900.

Die Balletttruppe der
New York Metropolitan
Opera bei einer Pause
in einem Proberaum
am Broadway,
September 1900.

Le corps de ballet du
New York Metropolitan
Opera fait une pause
dans les salles de
répétition de Broadway,
septembre 1900.

Tamara Karsavina
in costume for
Michel Fokine's
ballet *Le Pavillon
d'Armide*, 1909.
This was the year she
joined Diaghilev's
Ballets Russes.

Tamara Karsawina
in ihrem Kostüm
für das Ballett
Le Pavillon d'Armide
von Michel Fokine,
1909. In diesem
Jahr wurde sie in
Diaghilews Ballett-
kompanie Ballets
Russes aufgenommen.

Tamara Karsavina en
costume pour le ballet
de Michel Fokine,
Le Pavillon d'Armide,
1909. La même
année, elle rejoignit
les Ballets russes
de Diaghilev.

Anna Pavlova and Mikhail Mordkin, c. 1900. Mordkin had just become first soloist with the Bolshoi Company. Pavlova was barely 16 years old.

Anna Pawlowa und Michail Mordkin, um 1900. Mordkin war gerade erster Solotänzer des Bolschoitheaters geworden. Pawlowa war gerade 16 Jahre alt.

Anna Pavlova et Mikhail Mordkin, vers 1900. Mordkin venait d'accéder au titre de premier danseur de la compagnie du Bolshoï. Pavlova avait à peine 16 ans.

(Above) Towards the end of his career, the American writer Mark Twain relaxes over a game of billiards, c. 1900. (Opposite) The Irish poet W B Yeats, at the height of his poetic powers, January 1908.

(Oben) Gegen Ende seiner schöpferischen Laufbahn entspannt sich der Schriftsteller Mark Twain beim Billard, um 1900. (Gegenüberliegende Seite) Der irische Dichter W. B. Yeats auf dem Höhepunkt seines dichterischen Schaffens, Januar 1908.

(Ci-dessus) Vers la fin de sa carrière, l'écrivain américain Mark Twain se détend en jouant au billard, vers 1900. (Ci-contre) Le poète irlandais W. B. Yeats à l'apogée de son talent créateur, janvier 1908.

The Italian tenor
Enrico Caruso,
photographed just
before his first
visits to London
and New York in
1902 and 1903
respectively.

Der italienische Tenor
Enrico Caruso, kurz
vor seinen ersten
Aufenthalten in
London (1902) und
New York (1903).

Le ténor italien
Enrico Caruso,
photographié juste
avant ses premières
visites à Londres
et New York,
respectivement en
1902 et 1903.

The Australian soprano Nellie Melba in the role of Marguerite in *Faust*, c. 1900. She had yet to inspire the pudding, sauce or toast named after her.

Die australische Sopranistin Nellie Melba in der Rolle des Gretchen in *Faust*, um 1900. Der süßen Nachspeise, der Soße und dem Toastbrot, die nach ihr benannt wurden, sollte sie erst zu späterer Zeit zu deren Namen verhelfen.

La soprano australienne Nellie Melba dans le rôle de la Marguerite de *Faust*, vers 1900. Elle n'avait pas encore inspiré le dessert et la sauce qui portent son nom.

Count Leo Nikolayevich Tolstoy and his wife Sonya, c. 1905. He lived his last years as a peasant, having denounced wealth and religion as well as his own works.

Graf Lew Nikolajewitsch Tolstoj und seine Frau Sonja, um 1905. Seine letzten Jahre verbrachte er als armer Bauer, nachdem er Reichtum, Religion und auch seine eigenen Werke verworfen hatte.

Le comte Léon Tolstoï et son épouse Sonia, vers 1905. Il vécut ses dernières années en paysan, ayant dénoncé l'argent et la religion et renié son œuvre.

The novelist and playwright Maxim Gorky (centre, white beard) with the cast of *Smug Citizens*, 1902. It was the year he wrote his greatest play, *The Lower Depths*. He was increasingly involved in the revolutionary movement.

Der Romanschriftsteller und Dramatiker Maksim Gorkij (Mitte, mit weißem Bart) inmitten der Schauspielerbesetzung des Stückes *Die Kleinbürger,* 1902. In diesem Jahr schrieb er sein bedeutendstes Theaterstück, *Nachtasyl.* Immer stärker war er auch an der revolutionären Bewegung beteiligt.

Le romancier et dramaturge Maxime Gorki (au centre, avec une barbe blanche) avec la distribution des *Petits-Bourgeois,* 1902. Cette année-là, il écrivit sa plus grande pièce, *Les Bas-Fonds.* Il s'impliqua de plus en plus dans le mouvement révolutionnaire.

A study of the Austrian composer Gustav Mahler, c. 1907, the year he resigned as conductor of the Vienna State Opera.

Eine Studie des österreichischen Komponisten Gustav Mahler, um 1907. In diesem Jahr trat er vom Amt des Dirigenten an der Wiener Staatsoper zurück.

Étude du compositeur autrichien Gustav Mahler, vers 1907, l'année où ce dernier démissionna de son poste de chef d'orchestre à l'Opéra national de Vienne.

The French composer Claude Debussy, c. 1909. By this time, he was devoting his talents almost entirely to chamber and piano music.

Der französische Komponist Claude Debussy, um 1909. Zu dieser Zeit widmete er sich fast ausschließlich der Klavier- und der Kammermusik.

Le compositeur français Claude Debussy, vers 1909. À cette époque, il se consacrait presque entièrement à la musique de chambre et pour piano.

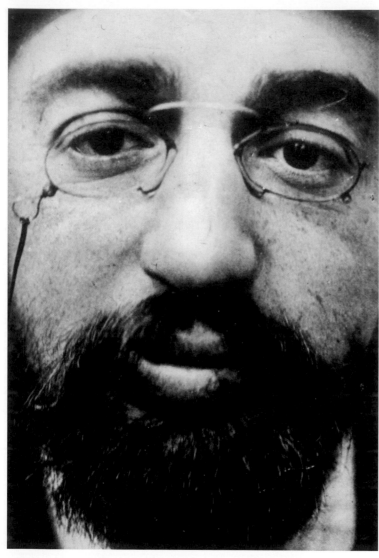

The French painter
Henri de Toulouse-
Lautrec in 1900.
His alcoholism had
induced a complete
breakdown, and
he had only a
year to live.

Der französische
Maler Henri de
Toulouse-Lautrec,
1900. Sein Alko-
holismus führte
zu seinem völligen
Zusammenbruch.
Ein Jahr später
starb er.

Le peintre français
Henri de Toulouse-
Lautrec, 1900. Son
alcoolisme avait pro-
voqué un complet
effondrement et il
n'avait plus qu'une
année à vivre.

There was, however, still plenty of life left in Pierre-Auguste
Renoir, though his hands were becoming crippled with arthritis.
He is seen here with friends at his house in Les Collettes, Cagnes,
in 1905.

Pierre-Auguste Renoir hingegen hatte noch ein langes Leben vor
sich, obwohl seine Hände durch Arthritis verkrüppelt waren.
Hier sieht man ihn mit Freunden in seinem Haus in Les Collettes,
Cagnes, 1905.

Pierre-Auguste Renoir au contraire était encore plein de vitalité,
même si ses mains étaient paralysées par l'arthrite. On le voit ici
avec des amis dans sa villa Les Collettes à Cagnes, 1905.

Three of Eadweard Muybridge's magnificent pictures of the American dancer Isadora Duncan, c. 1900. Just as Muybridge revolutionised action photography, so Duncan revolutionised dance.

Drei großartige Aufnahmen der amerikanischen Tänzerin Isadora Duncan von Eadweard Muybridge, um 1900. So wie Muybridge die Bewegungsfotografie revolutioniert hatte, so hatte Duncan den Tanz revolutioniert.

Trois des magnifiques images de la danseuse Isadora Duncan réalisées par Eadweard Muybridge, vers 19 Tout comme Muybridge révolutio nait la photographie du mouvemer Duncan révolutionnait la danse.

The boy who never grew up – and his creator. (Opposite) Stephanie Stephens as Peter Pan in a 1906 production of J M Barrie's most famous play. (Right) Barrie with Miss A N Emery.

Der Junge – der niemals erwachsen wurde – und sein schöpferischer Vater. (Gegenüberliegende Seite) Stephanie Stephens als Peter Pan in einer Inszenierung von J. M. Barries berühmtestem Theaterstück im Jahre 1906. (Rechts) Barrie mit Miss A. N. Emery.

Le garçon qui ne voulait pas grandir … et son créateur. (Ci-contre) Stephanie Stephens jouant Peter Pan dans une production de la célébrissime pièce de J. M. Barrie, en 1906. (À droite) Barrie avec Miss A. N. Emery.

(Above) The French sculptor Auguste Rodin in his museum at Meudon, c. 1909.
(Opposite) Youth pays light-hearted homage to Edgar Degas (seated, centre),
c. 1900. Almost blind, the great man could barely see the camera.

(Oben) Der französische Bildhauer Auguste Rodin in seinem Museum in Meudon,
um 1909. (Gegenüberliegende Seite) Jugendliche erweisen Edgar Degas
(Mitte, sitzend) die Ehre, um 1900. Da er fast blind war, konnte der berühmte
Mann kaum die Kamera sehen.

(Ci-dessus) Le sculpteur français Auguste Rodin dans son musée à Meudon,
vers 1909. (Ci-contre) La jeunesse rendant un hommage un peu léger à Edgar
Degas (assis, au centre), vers 1900. Étant presque aveugle, le peintre pouvait
difficilement distinguer l'appareil photo.

The principal speaker at this protest meeting against a visit to London
by Tsar Nicholas in 1908 was George Bernard Shaw (centre, without hat).
It was Shaw's proud boast that he was an 'immoralist and heretic'.

Der wichtigste Redner bei dieser Protestkundgebung gegen den Besuch
des Zaren Nikolaus in London im Jahre 1908 war George Bernard Shaw
(Mitte, ohne Hut). Shaw war besonders stolz auf seine „unmoralische
und ketzerische" Haltung.

L'orateur principal, à ce meeting de protestation contre une visite
à Londres du tsar Nicolas en 1908, était George Bernard Shaw
(au centre, sans chapeau). Shaw se flattait d'être à la fois « immoraliste »
et « hérétique ».

Adeline Virginia Stephen (Virginia Woolf) with her father, Sir Leslie
Stephen, in 1902. Two years later, her father died and she moved
to Bloomsbury where she took up writing. The rest is a stream
of consciousness.

Adeline Virginia Stephen (Virginia Woolf) mit ihrem Vater, Sir Leslie
Stephen, im Jahre 1902. Zwei Jahre später starb ihr Vater, und sie
zog nach Bloomsbury. Dort begann sie zu schreiben. Alles Weitere
ist Geschichte.

Adeline Virginia Stephen (Virginia Woolf) avec son père, Sir Leslie
Stephen, en 1902. Deux ans plus tard, son père mourut et elle s'installa
à Bloomsbury où elle se mit à écrire. Le reste appartient à l'histoire.

10. Fashion
Mode
La mode

The classic hourglass figure. It was the invention of the American illustrator Charles Dana Gibson, and those who forced their bodies into this shape were known as 'Gibson Girls'. Camille Clifford, the owner of this particular classic, was a Danish-born actress.

Die klassische Sanduhrenfigur. Eine Erfindung des amerikanischen Illustrators Charles Dana Gibson. Die so genannten „Gibson Girls" zwangen ihren Körper in diese Form. Camille Clifford, die das Ideal dieser besonderen klassischen Form darstellte, war eine in Dänemark geborene Schauspielerin.

La silhouette classique dite en « sablier » fut inventée par l'illustrateur américain Charles Dana Gibson ; celles qui imposaient cette forme à leur corps étaient appelées les « Gibson Girls ». Camille Clifford, propriétaire de cette classique plastique, était une actrice d'origine danoise.

10. Fashion
Mode
La mode

The gloom and restrictions of Victorian times were swept aside by the fashion of the early 1900s. There was a wealth of beautiful materials – velvets, taffetas, *crêpes de Chine*, the softest of wool, the smoothest of cotton, the most delicious silks. There was a wealth of beautiful colour – creams and pinks, flaming reds and deep blues, the gentlest of lilac, the lightest of lavender, and greys that shone with the lustre of silver. There was a plethora of exquisite design – sleeves that dripped with elegance, skirts that hung with grace and style.

There was wealth. There was beauty. Fashion was expensive. Only the rich could afford the abundance of lace and fur, the trimmings of pearl and jet, the threads of gold and the coronets of glimmering jewels. The middle classes starched their cuffs and collars, had their shoes shined and did what they could with cunning and artifice to emulate their well-draped betters. The poor darned and mended their own clothes, and wore their fingers to the bone to make the gorgeous clothes that only the rich would wear.

But the parade of wealth and beauty continued. Actresses, dowagers, débutantes, society beauties and rich young heiresses made sure that they were seen at race meetings, balls, receptions, first nights and photographers' studios in their immaculate and glorious attire.

Die düstere Atmosphäre des viktorianischen Zeitalters wurde mit der Mode des frühen 20. Jahrhunderts vertrieben. Es gab eine Fülle an wundervollen Materialien – Samtstoffe, Taft, Crêpe de Chine, weiche Woll- und glatte Baumwollstoffe und herrlichste Seide. Dann gab es die vielfältigsten und wunderschönsten Farben – Cremefarben, Rosatöne, leuchtendes Rot und tiefdunkles Blau, die zartesten Lilaschattierungen, hellste Lavendelfarben und Grautöne, die silbrig schimmerten. Viele ausgewählte Schnitte standen zur Verfügung – elegant herabhängende Ärmel, anmutig und stilvoll die Beine umschmeichelnde Röcke.

Vielfalt und Schönheit bestimmten die aufwändige Mode. Doch nur die Reichen konnten sich die zahllosen Spitzen und Pelze, mit Perlen und Gagat besetzte Accessoires, Brokatstickereien und mit glitzernden Juwelen besetzte Krönchen leisten. Die Leute des Mittelstandes stärkten ihre Manschetten und Kragen, ließen ihre Schuhe putzen und improvisierten mit List und Geschick, um den betuchteren Leuten nachzueifern. Die armen Leute stopften und flickten ihre Kleidung selbst und nähten sich an den prächtigen Kleidern für die Reichen die Finger wund.

Die Reichen und Schönen ließen keine Gelegenheit aus, sich zur Schau zu stellen. Schauspielerinnen, adlige Witwen, Debütantinnen, die Schönen der Gesellschaft und junge reiche Erbinnen achteten darauf, dass sie auf Rennveranstaltungen, Bällen, Empfängen, Premieren und in Fotoateliers in ihren makellosen und herrlichen Kleidern auch gesehen wurden.

La tristesse et la sévérité de l'ère victorienne furent balayées par la mode du début des années 1900. Ce fut une abondance de matières : velours, taffetas, crêpes de Chine, les laines les plus douces, les cotons les plus souples, les soies les plus délicates. Ce fut une profusion de couleurs : des crèmes, des roses, des rouges enflammés et des bleus profonds, les mauves les plus tendres, les bleus lavande les plus vaporeux et des gris brillants. Ce fut une pléthore de lignes exquises : des manches élégantes et fluides, des jupes tombant gracieusement.

Il y avait de la richesse, de la beauté et la mode était chère. Seuls les riches pouvaient s'offrir le luxe de la dentelle et de la fourrure, les parures de perles et de jais, les fils d'or et les diadèmes sertis d'étincelants joyaux. La classe moyenne amidonnait ses cols et ses manchettes, lustrait ses chaussures et faisait ce qu'elle pouvait pour imiter l'élégance des plus aisés. Les pauvres reprisaient et raccomodaient leurs habits tout en usant leurs doigts à coudre et à broder les magnifiques toilettes que seuls les riches pouvaient porter.

Mais la parade de la richesse et de la beauté continuait. Actrices, douairières, débutantes, beautés mondaines et jeunes héritières ne manquaient pas de s'afficher aux courses, aux bals, aux réceptions, aux premières et dans les studios des photographes, parées de leurs atours glorieux et immaculés …

(Left) The French actress Gaby Deslys who brought American fashion to Europe. (Opposite) The extravagance of the Folies Bergère, 1905.

(Links) Die französische Schauspielerin Gaby Deslys, die die amerikanische Mode nach Europa brachte. (Gegenüberliegende Seite) Die Extravaganz des Folies Bergère, 1905.

(À gauche) L'actrice française Gaby Deslys, qui introduisit en Europe la mode américaine. (Ci-contre) L'extravagance des Folies Bergère, 1905.

In Edwardian times, women's fashions became less bulky and more manageable. This suited their more active lifestyle. It would have been impossible, 50 years earlier, to play croquet in a crinoline.

Zur Zeit Edwards VII. wurde die Damenmode leichter und war somit einfacher zu handhaben. Dies passte besser zum aktiven Leben der Frauen. In einem Reifrock Krocket zu spielen, wäre 50 Jahre zuvor nicht möglich gewesen.

Sous le règne d'Édouard VII, la mode féminine devint moins encombrante, plus facile à porter et mieux adaptée à un style de vie plus actif. 50 ans plus tôt, il eût été impossible de jouer au croquet en crinoline.

The 6th Earl Spencer and his son, Lord Althorp, step out. It was an age when men shone with smartness. Top hats, shoes, lapels, even the ferrules of their umbrellas gleamed. Women had softer styles in sumptuous materials.

Der 6. Earl Spencer und sein Sohn, Lord Althorp, gehen aus. Zu dieser Zeit bestachen Männer durch ihr gepflegtes Äußeres. Ihre Zylinder, Schuhe, Revers und sogar die Knäufe ihrer Schirme glänzten. Der Stil der Damenmode und ihre exquisiten Materialien waren „weicher".

Le 6ᵉ comte Spencer et son fils, Lord Althorp, marchant d'un bon pas. À cette époque, les hommes ne manquaient pas d'allure. Chapeaux hauts-de-forme, chaussures, revers, même le manche du parapluie brillait. Les femmes avaient une élégance plus douce, faite de somptueuses matières.

The voluptuous Edwardian figure was seen to its full advantage on stage. Here are four members of the chorus from *The Dairymaids*, 24 April 1906.

Die sinnlich üppige Figur zur Zeit Edwards VII. wurde in voller Pracht auf der Bühne gezeigt. Hier sieht man vier Damen der Tanzgruppe aus *The Dairymaids*, 24. April 1906.

La silhouette voluptueuse de l'époque édouardienne semblait toute faite pour la scène. Ici, quatre membres du chœur du spectacle *The Dairymaids*, 24 avril 1906.

(Opposite) The actor Sydney Barraclough, c. 1909. To wear a clean white suit needed a hard-working valet in an age of city smut and grime. (Above) Leslie Stiles and Camille Clifford in a scene from *The Belle of Mayfair*, 11 April 1906.

(Gegenüberliegende Seite) Der Schauspieler Sydney Barraclough, um 1909. Um einen sauberen weißen Anzug tragen zu können, brauchte man in einer Zeit, in der Schmutz und Dreck die Stadt beherrschten, einen emsigen Kammerdiener. (Oben) Leslie Stiles und Camille Clifford in einer Szene aus *The Belle of Mayfair*, 11. April 1906.

(Ci-contre) L'acteur Sydney Barraclough, vers 1909. Porter un costume blanc impeccable exigeait les services d'un valet dévoué, à une époque où les villes étaient pleines de poussière et de crasse. (Ci-dessus) Leslie Stiles et Camille Clifford dans une scène de *The Belle of Mayfair*, 11 avril 1906.

Dressed against the
elements. (Opposite)
Three well-covered
paddlers, and (right)
a Welsh bathing belle
on the beach
at Swansea.

Bademode.
(Gegenüberliegende
Seite) Drei gut
verpackte Badegäste
und (rechts) eine
walisische Bade-
schönheit am Strand
von Swansea.

Parés contre les
éléments. (Ci-contre)
Trois barboteurs
bien couverts et
(à droite) une naïade
galloise sur la plage
de Swansea

Children were often overdressed. (Left) A young boy in suit and Eton collar, 1900. (Opposite) Miss Kennedy Stott in full regalia, 6 May 1904.

Kinder waren häufig übertrieben schick gekleidet. (Links) Ein kleiner Junge im Anzug mit breitem Umlegekragen, 1900. (Gegenüberliegende Seite) Miss Kennedy Stott in voller Pracht, 6. Mai 1904.

Les enfants étaient souvent vêtus avec trop de recherche. (À gauche) Un petit garçon en costume et grand col dur, 1900. (Ci-contre) Miss Kennedy Stott en grande toilette, 6 mai 1904.

Carl and Mark Neaver de Monte in their school uniforms, May 1902. Children well down the social scale worn similar clothes for school, adding discomfort to discipline.

Carl und Mark Neaver de Monte in ihren Schuluniformen, Mai 1902. Die Kinder aller gesellschaftlichen Schichten trugen die gleiche Kleidung in der Schule. Dies war zusätzlich zur Disziplin auch noch unbequem.

Carl et Mark Neaver de Monte en uniforme de classe, mai 1902. Les enfants appartenant à des classes sociales bien inférieures devaient eux aussi porter des uniformes comparables à l'école, ajoutant l'inconfort à la discipline.

But even at home there was little notion of casual clothes. Master Trotter poses for George C Beresford's camera in an informal suit, April 1902.

Sogar zu Hause gab es kaum eine Vorstellung von Freizeitkleidung. Herr Trotter steht in einem legeren Anzug Modell vor George C. Beresfords Kamera, April 1902.

Mais même à la maison, on accordait peu d'importance au confort. Le jeune sieur Trotter, en costume informel, pose pour l'appareil de George C. Beresford, avril 1902.

Even the stiffest of sea breezes would have taken some time to dry these voluminous bathing costumes. In 1909, however, they were the last word in seaside chic, attracting many a roguish eye when filled.

Selbst bei der steifsten Brise dauerte es einige Zeit, bis diese riesigen Badeanzüge trockneten. 1909 waren sie jedoch der letzte Schrei in der Bademode und zogen so manchen verstohlenen Blick auf sich.

Même la plus rude des brises marines aurait mis du temps à sécher ces volumineux costumes de bain. En 1909 cependant, ils étaient du dernier chic et valaient à celles qui les portaient plus d'un regard émoustillé.

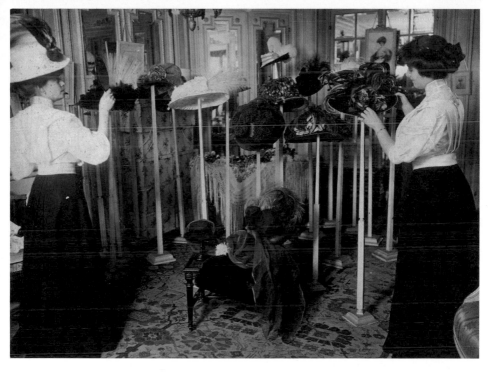

A selection of hats from Maison Corbier at the Exposition des Chapeaux in Paris, 1905. A lady would never be seen without a striking hat. A bare head was a sign of the 'new woman', one who liked both to smoke and vote.

Eine Auswahl an Hüten des Maison Corbier auf der Hutmesse in Paris, 1905. Eine Dame wäre nie ohne einen auffallenden Hut auf die Straße gegangen. Ging man ohne Kopfbedeckung vor die Tür, so war dies ein Zeichen dafür, dass man eine moderne Frau war, die gerne rauchte und zur Wahl ging.

Une sélection de chapeaux de la maison Corbier à l'Exposition des chapeaux de Paris, 1905. Une vraie dame ne sortait jamais sans un couvre-chef attirant le regard. Seules sortaient tête nue les « nouvelles femmes », celles qui voulaient aussi fumer et voter.

(Left) Memoirs of a foxhunting man. Colonel Douglas Brooke, Master of Foxhounds, 1 May 1902. (Opposite) The actress Phyllis Dare favours ermine, 1905.

(Links) Memoiren eines Meisters der Fuchsjagd. Colonel Douglas Brooke, Fuchsjagdmeister, 1. Mai 1902. (Gegenüberliegende Seite) Die Schauspielerin Phyllis Dare liebt Hermelin, 1905.

(À gauche) Le colonel Douglas Brooke, grand maître dans l'art de la chasse au renard, 1ᵉʳ mai 1902. (Ci-contre) L'actrice Phyllis Dare préférait l'hermine, 1905.

11. Science
Wissenschaft
Les sciences

In modern terms it was merely a piece of communications
technology. To the early 20th century it was a wonder of
science that entered the home. (Right) The British actress
Iris Hoey poses beside the telephone, c. 1909.

Heutzutage ist es ein selbstverständlicher Bestandteil der
Kommunikationstechnologie. Zu Beginn des 20. Jahrhunderts
aber war es ein Wunder der Wissenschaft, das seinen Einzug
in die privaten Haushalte hielt. (Rechts) Die britische Schauspielerin Iris Hoey posiert neben dem Telefon, um 1909.

Aujourd'hui on se contenterait de parler de technologie de
communication. Pour le XXe siècle naissant, il s'agissait d'une
merveille de la science faisant son entrée dans les foyers.
(À droite) L'actrice britannique Iris Hoey pose devant un
téléphone, vers 1909.

11. Science
Wissenschaft
Les sciences

Electric-powered machines hummed away, valves flickered, retorts bubbled over the gas jets of Bunsen burners, named after the German chemist who died in 1899. In the early 1900s, research and discovery were in the hands of men and women working at home, in small laboratories with equipment they had made, and on ideas that were their own. And such ideas! In 1900 Max Planck revolutionised physics with the publication of his quantum theory of energy. Five years later Albert Einstein applied Planck's ideas to light and produced his theory of relativity. In 1906 Marie Curie succeeded her husband Pierre as Professor of Physics at the Sorbonne, but much of the work on radium for which they were awarded the Nobel Prize for Physics in 1903 had been done after hours, or at home.

Nations were just beginning to realise how important science was, how carefully scientists should be nurtured, how much investment was needed in new institutes of higher education, how the race was on to be the first, the smartest, the most advanced. Science was becoming a weapon, and gradually the little workshops with their home-made equipment would make way for the gleaming laboratories of large corporations.

Elektrisch betriebene Maschinen surrten, Röhren flimmerten, Retorten brodelten über der Flamme eines Bunsenbrenners, benannt nach dem deutschen Chemiker Bunsen, der im Jahre 1899 starb. Anfang des 20. Jahrhunderts lag die Forschung und Entdeckung von Neuheiten vor allem in den Händen von Männern und Frauen, die zu Hause in kleinen Labors mit selbst gebastelter Ausrüstung an ihren eigenen Ideen experimentierten und arbeiteten. Und was für Ideen dies waren! 1900 revolutionierte Max Planck die Physik mit der Veröffentlichung seiner Quantentheorie. Fünf Jahre später wandte Albert Einstein die Idee von Planck auf das Licht an und entwarf seine Relativitätstheorie. 1906 löste Marie Curie ihren Ehemann

Pierre als Professorin für Physik an der Sorbonne ab. Doch ein Großteil ihrer Arbeit für die Entdeckung von Radium, für die ihnen 1903 der Nobelpreis für Physik verliehen wurde, fand nach den Vorlesungen oder bei ihnen zu Hause statt.

Auf der Welt wurde man sich gerade erst bewusst, welch bedeutende Rolle der Wissenschaft zukam, mit welcher Sorgfalt man die Wissenschaftler ausbilden musste und welche Investitionen für neue Hochschulinstitute nötig waren. Man erkannte, dass der Mensch auf dem Weg war, die höchste, klügste und fortschrittlichste Spezies zu werden. Die Wissenschaft entwickelte sich langsam zu einem Machtinstrument. Allmählich wichen die kleinen Werkstätten mit ihrer selbst gebastelten Ausrüstung den hervorragend ausgestatteten Labors großer Handelsgesellschaften.

Les machines électriques bourdonnaient, les soupapes dansaient, les cornues bouillonnaient sur les flammes au gaz des becs Bunsen, du nom du chimiste allemand mort en 1899. Au début des années 1900, la recherche et les découvertes étaient faites par des hommes et des femmes qui travaillaient chez eux, dans de petits laboratoires équipés tant bien que mal, et suivant des idées qui étaient les leurs. Et quelles idées! En 1900, Max Planck révolutionna la physique en publiant sa théorie quantique de l'énergie. Cinq ans plus tard, Albert Einstein appliquait les idées de Planck à la lumière, donnant naissance à la théorie de la relativité. En 1906, Marie Curie succédait à son mari Pierre à la chaire de physique de la Sorbonne, mais la majeure partie des recherches sur le radium, pour lesquelles ils avaient reçu le prix Nobel en 1903, avaient été réalisées après les heures de travail, ou à la maison.

Dans tous les pays on commençait à peine à comprendre l'importance de la science, le soin à apporter à la formation des scientifiques, la nécessité d'investir dans de nouvelles institutions d'enseignement supérieur, la réalité de la course engagée pour être le premier, le plus intelligent, le plus avancé. La science devenait une arme et progressivement les petits ateliers avec leurs équipements artisanaux firent place aux laboratoires rutilants des grandes compagnies.

Guglielmo Marconi
(extreme left)
watches the prepa-
ration of the kite that
received the first
transatlantic telegraph
signals, St John's,
Newfoundland,
12 December 1907.

Guglielmo Marconi
(links außen) beob-
achtet den Aufbau
des Drachens, der
die ersten transatlan-
tischen telegrafischen
Signale empfing,
St. John's,
Neufundland,
12. Dezember 1907.

Guglielmo Marconi
(à l'extrême gauche)
surveille la prépara-
tion du cerf-volant
destiné à recevoir
les premiers signaux
télégraphiques trans-
atlantiques. St John's,
Terre-Neuve,
12 décembre 1907.

Employees at the Marconi Wireless Telegraph factory in Chelmsford
assemble decremeters and wave meters, c. 1909. Marconi's invention
was an enormous and immediate financial success.

Angestellte der Marconi Rundfunkfabrik in Chelmsford bauen
Dämpfungs- und Wellenmessgeräte zusammen, um 1909. Marconis
Erfindung der drahtlosen Telegrafie war ein großartiger und rascher
finanzieller Erfolg.

Des employés de l'usine de « télégraphe sans fil » de Marconi à Chelmsford
assemblent des oscillateurs et des ondemètres, vers 1909. L'invention de
Marconi fut immédiatement un immense succès financier.

As the telephone and telegraph networks spread, the world was knitted together with a web of wires. An engineer fixes overhead telephone cables above London's Fleet Street, 1907.

Die Telefon- und Telegrafennetze wuchsen unaufhörlich. So wurde die Welt mit Drähten vernetzt. Ein Techniker befestigt Telefonkabel über der Fleet Street in London, 1907.

L'extension rapide des connexions téléphoniques et télégraphiques fit que le monde entier fut bientôt parcouru par un réseau de fils. Un technicien fixe des câbles téléphoniques en altitude au-dessus de Fleet Street, Londres, 1907.

The first picture transmitted by wire in Germany, 16 May 1907. It was of Emperor Wilhelm II. The transmission took six minutes.

Das erste Bild, das durch einen Draht übertragen wurde, Deutschland, 16. Mai 1907. Es zeigt Kaiser Wilhelm II. Die Übertragung dauerte sechs Minuten.

La première image transmise par câble en Allemagne, le 16 mai 1907. Il s'agit de l'empereur Guillaume II. La transmission dura 6 minutes.

The Empire comes together, January 1909. A telegraph operator in London receives a message from India.

Das Empire rückt zusammen, Januar 1909. Ein Telegrafist in London empfängt eine Nachricht aus Indien.

L'empire britannique en liaison, janvier 1909. À Londres, un opérateur du télégraphe décripte un message parti d'Inde.

Early protection against the perils of fire fighting. A member of the London Fire Brigade with a smoke helmet, 1908.

Damaliger Schutz vor Gefahren bei der Brandbekämpfung. Ein Mitglied der Londoner Feuerwehr mit einer Rauchmaske, 1908.

Premiers dispositifs de protection des soldats du feu. Un membre de la brigade des pompiers de Londres, équipé d'un casque anti-fumée, 1908.

Three members of a colliery rescue team with safety lamps and Draeger smoke helmets, 1 March 1908. It was a time of appalling mining disasters all over the world; before long, gas masks would be needed above ground.

Drei Mitglieder einer Grubenrettungsmannschaft mit Grubenlampen und Dräger-Rauchmasken, 1. März 1908. Zu dieser Zeit ereigneten sich auf der ganzen Welt schreckliche Grubenunglücke. Bald sollten Gasmasken auch über Tage zum Einsatz kommen.

Trois membres d'une équipe de secours miniers équipés de lampes de sécurité et de casques anti-fumée Draeger, 1ᵉʳ mars 1908. Cette époque connaissait d'épouvantables catastrophes minières à travers le monde ; mais bientôt, des masques à gaz seraient nécessaires également à la surface du sol.

Reinhold Thiele's picture of a woman inside an electric bath at the Light Care Institute, London, c. 1900. The bath was a heavyweight version of a modern sun-bed, and was used for medical reasons.

Reinhold Thieles Foto von einer Frau in einem elektrischen Wannenbad im Light Care Institute, London, um 1900. Diese Wanne war der schwergewichtige Vorläufer der heutigen Sonnenbank und wurde für medizinische Zwecke verwendet.

Photo, par Reinhold Thiele, d'une femme à l'intérieur d'une baignoire électrique au Light Care Institute, Londres, vers 1900. C'était une sorte de version lourde d'un appareil à ultra-violets et ce traitement était prescrit dans un cadre médical.

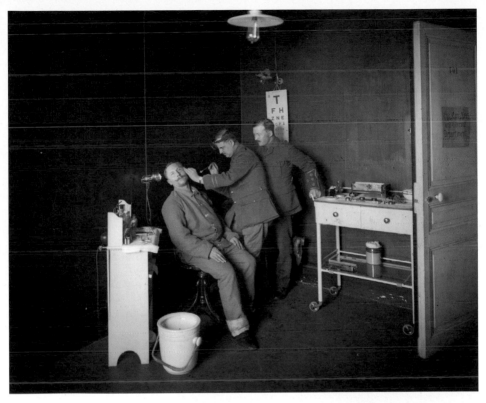

An army hearing test photographed by Thiele, c. 1905. It may be that Tommy Atkins has suffered damage from the noise of an exploding gun, or simply that recruits now faced a more rigorous medical before being accepted.

Ein Hörtest bei der Armee, aufgenommen von Thiele, um 1905. Möglicherweise hatte Tommy Atkins von dem Lärm einer explodierenden Kanone Schäden davongetragen, oder die Rekruten mussten sich nun einer strengeren ärztlichen Kontrolle unterziehen, bevor sie in die Armee aufgenommen wurden.

Test de l'ouïe à l'armée, photographie de Thiele, vers 1905. Peut-être l'oreille interne du soldat avait-elle souffert du bruit d'une explosion trop proche, ou simplement les nouvelles recrues devaient-elles se plier à des examens médicaux plus rigoureux qu'auparavant.

The German-born mathematical physicist Albert Einstein, 1905. It was the year of the publication of his theory of relativity.

Der in Deutschland geborene Physiker Albert Einstein, 1905. In dem Jahr veröffentlichte er seine Relativitätstheorie.

Albert Einstein, physicien et mathématicien né en Allemagne, 1905. Cette photographie date de l'année de sa théorie de la relativité.

The Polish-born
physicist Marie Curie
in her laboratory
in Paris, c. 1909.
She was working
on the isolation of
pure radium.

Die in Polen
geborene Physikerin
Marie Curie in ihrem
Labor in Paris, um
1909. Sie arbeitete
daran, reines Radium
zu isolieren.

Marie Curie,
d'origine polonaise,
dans son laboratoire
à Paris, vers 1909.
Elle travaillait à isoler
du radium pur.

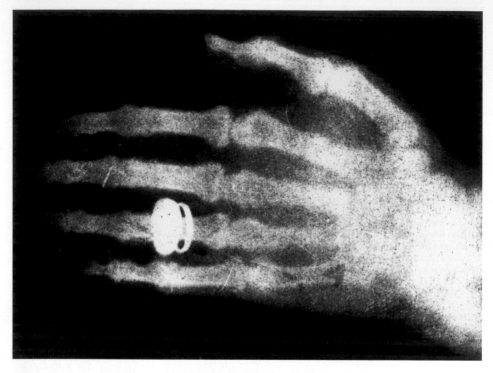

(Opposite) The German physicist Wilhelm Conrad Röntgen, 1906.
His discovery of X-rays won him the Nobel Prize for Physics in 1901.
(Above) One of Röntgen's first X-ray pictures – his wife's hand.

(Gegenüberliegende Seite) Der deutsche Physiker Wilhelm Conrad
Röntgen, 1906. Für seine Entdeckung der Röntgenstrahlen erhielt er
1901 den Nobelpreis für Physik. (Oben) Eine der ersten Aufnahmen
von Röntgen – die Hand seiner Frau.

(Ci-contre) Le physicien allemand Wilhelm Conrad Röntgen, 1906.
Sa découverte des rayons X lui valut le prix Nobel de physique en
1901. (Ci-dessus) L'un des premiers clichés aux rayons X de Röntgen :
la main de sa femme.

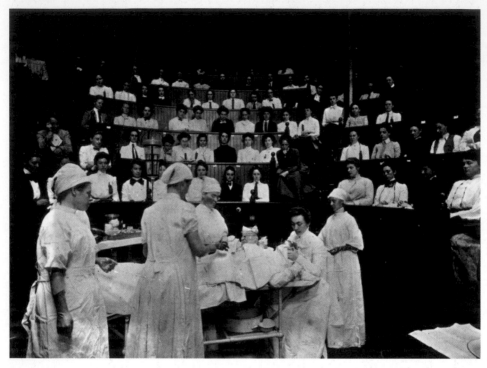

Florence Nightingale takes over. American women doctors perform an
operation in front of a lecture theatre full of students, November 1907.
Some men were amused, others horrified. The patient was grateful.

Florence Nightingale bei der Arbeit. Amerikanische Ärztinnen führen
vor Studenten in einem gefüllten Vorlesungssaal eine Operation durch,
November 1907. Einige Männer waren belustigt, andere entsetzt.
Der Patient war dankbar.

Florence Nightingale reprend la main. Des doctoresses américaines
opèrent devant un amphithéâtre rempli d'étudiants. Certains hommes
étaient amusés, d'autres horrifiés. Le patient fut reconnaissant.

A medical assistant
in protective
clothing prepares
to take an X-ray,
March 1909. The
patient was terrified.

Ein Assistenzarzt in
einem Schutzanzug
trifft Vorbereitungen
für eine Röntgenauf-
nahme, März 1909.
Der Patient hatte
schreckliche Angst.

Un assistant médical,
dans un attirail de
protection, se
prépare à prendre un
cliché aux rayons X,
mars 1909. Le
patient fut terrifié.

The Lavery Electric Automatic Phrenometer whirrs into action, August 1907. It measured the activity of the brain. This is the portable version.

Der automatische elektrische Gehirn-strommesser von Lavery fängt an zu surren, August 1907. Damit konnte man die Gehirnaktivität messen. Hier sieht man die mobile Ausführung.

Le « phrénomètre électrique et auto-matique » de Lavery entre en action, août 1907. Il servait à mesurer l'activité du cerveau. Ceci est la version portable de l'appareil.

A penny-in-the-slot
boot and shoe-
polishing machine,
November 1907.
It was noisier than
a boot boy but did
not require a tip.

Ein Schuhputz-
automat, November
1907. Er war lauter
als ein Schuhputz-
junge, verlangte aber
kein Trinkgeld.

Une machine-à-
sous-à-cirer-les-
chaussures,
novembre 1907.
Plus bruyante qu'un
cireur ambulant,
elle n'attendait pas
de pourboire.

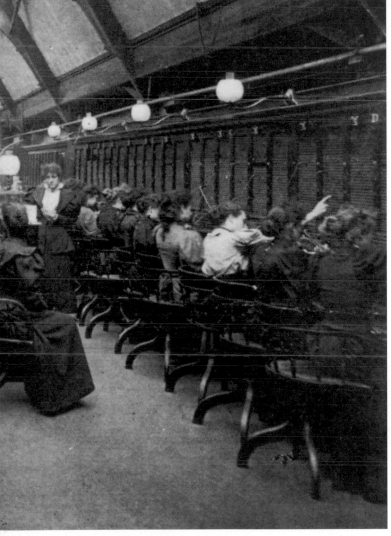

Switchboard
operators at the
Manchester
Telephone Exchange,
c. 1900. The super-
visors are seated in
the centre aisle.

Telefonistinnen der
Vermittlungsstelle
Manchester,
um 1900. Die
Aufseherinnen sitzen
im Mittelgang.

Les opératrices de la
centrale téléphonique
de Manchester, vers
1900. Les personnes
assises au milieu
supervisent le travail.

12. Transport
Verkehr
Les moyens de transport

A brief period of co-existence before the New drove the Old off the road. A motor cab overtakes a horse-drawn hansom on a city street, July 1907. The days of nipping into the road for a shovelful of manure for the garden were numbered.

Bevor die neuen Transportmittel die alten von der Straße verdrängten, gab es für kurze Zeit ein Nebeneinander. Ein Automobil überholt eine von einem Pferd gezogene Hansom (zweirädrige Kutsche) auf einer städtischen Straße, Juli 1907. Die Tage, in denen man für eine Schaufel voll Dung für den Garten auf die Straße flitzte, waren gezählt.

Une brève période de coexistence avant que l'ancien ne cède la place au nouveau. Un taxi automobile doublant un cab (cabriolet tiré par un cheval, dans lequel le cocher est assis à l'arrière) dans une rue urbaine, juillet 1907. Les jours étaient comptés, où l'on allait dans la rue se servir d'une pelletée de fumier pour engraisser le jardin.

12. Transport
   Verkehr
   Les moyens de transport

When the inaugural train opened the Paris Métro in 1900, it carried one passenger. There were no celebratory fireworks, no banquets, no speeches, no bands. One of the city's aldermen prophesied total failure for the scheme. He wondered who would want to use it.

Within a few years millions of passengers had allayed his fears. They flocked to the Métro as they did to the new Berlin Underground in 1902, the extensions to the London system, and the New York City subway in 1904. Above ground too, all was change. Railways enjoyed one last boom before they reached saturation point. There were electric buses, trams, taxis and elevated railways. Products of the great names in motoring – Daimler, Benz, Rolls and Royce, Panhard, De Dion, Ford, Renault and dozens more – hummed and rattled along the streets. Horse-drawn vehicles had a few more years in service, but the internal combustion engine was already master of the road.

Strange new contraptions took to the skies. The Wright brothers achieved the first flight by a heavier-than-air machine in 1903, three years after the first Zeppelin had loomed over Germany. Before the decade was out, Louis Blériot had flown over the Channel.

Bei der Jungfernfahrt der Pariser Metro im Jahre 1900 befand sich nur ein Fahrgast im Zug. Es gab kein feierliches Feuerwerk, kein Festessen, keine Reden, keine Musikkapelle. Einer der Herren aus dem Stadtrat prophezeite diesem Projekt einen Misserfolg auf der ganzen Linie. Er fragte sich, wer wohl diesen Zug benutzen würde.

Innerhalb weniger Jahre hatten Millionen von Fahrgästen seine Befürchtungen widerlegt. Sie strömten in die Metro genauso wie seit 1902 in die neue Berliner U-Bahn und 1904 in die ausgebauten Linien des Londoner Netzes und der New Yorker Subway. Auch über der Erde gab es große Veränderungen. Nach einem letzten Aufschwung hatte man genügend Eisenbahnen. Es gab elektrisch betriebene Busse, Straßenbahnen, Taxen und Hochbahnen. Die Markenfabrikate der Automobilbranche – Daimler, Benz, Rolls und Royce, Panhard, De Dion, Ford, Renault und viele mehr – brummten und ratterten durch die Straßen. Zwar waren die von Pferden gezogenen Fahrzeuge noch ein paar Jahre im Dienst, der Verbrennungsmotor hatte jedoch seinen Siegeszug auf der Straße bereits angetreten.

Sonderbare, neue Dinge erhoben sich in den Himmel. Die Gebrüder Wright vollbrachten im Jahre 1903 den ersten Flug mit einer Maschine, die schwerer als Luft war. Drei Jahre zuvor zeichnete sich der erste Zeppelin am Himmel über Deutschland ab. Bevor dieses Jahrzehnt zu Ende ging, war Louis Blériot über den Ärmelkanal geflogen.

Le premier métro qui démarra en 1900 ne comportait qu'un seul passager. Il n'y eut ni feux d'artifice, ni discours, ni musique. À cette époque, un conseiller municipal de la ville de Paris prophétisa un échec complet pour l'ensemble du plan. Il se demandait qui pourrait bien vouloir l'utiliser.

En quelques années, des millions de passagers dissipèrent ces craintes. Ils affluèrent dans le métro parisien comme ils le firent en 1902 dans celui de Berlin, dans les extensions du réseau londonien ou dans le subway de New York en 1904. En surface aussi, les choses changaient. Les chemins de fer vécurent une dernière phase de croissance exponentielle avant d'atteindre le point de saturation. Il y eut les bus électriques, les trams, les taxis et les rails aériens. Dans les rues, ronflaient et cahotaient les productions les plus récentes des grandes marques automobiles : Daimler, Benz, Rolls et Royce, Panhard, De Dion, Ford, Renault et des dizaines d'autres. Les voitures à cheval allaient encore servir pendant plusieurs années, mais déjà le moteur à combustion interne avait conquis les routes.

D'étranges objets volants envahissaient le ciel. Les frères Wright réussirent pour la première fois à faire voler un appareil plus lourd que l'air en 1903, trois ans après l'apparition du premier zeppelin dans le ciel allemand. Avant la fin de la décennie, Louis Blériot avait traversé la Manche.

Trademark of the 20th
century. Watched by his
brother Wilbur, Orville
Wright takes to the air in
his 12hp heavier-than-air
machine from the sands
of Kill Devil Hills, Kitty
Hawk, North Carolina,
17 December 1903.

Markenzeichen des
20. Jahrhunderts. Wilbur
sieht seinem Bruder Orville
Wright zu, als dieser mit
seinem 12-PS-Flugzeug von
den Sanddünen bei Kill Devil
Hills abhebt, Kitty Hawk,
North Carolina,
17. Dezember 1903.

La marque du XXe siècle.
Sous le regard de son frère
Wilbur, Orville Wright prend
son vol dans un appareil
12 CV plus lourd que l'air,
depuis les sables de Kill Devil
Hills, Kitty Hawk, Caroline-
du-Nord, 17 décembre 1903.

Touring the towers. (Opposite) The Italian airship *Parsival* is moored to the Campanile in the Piazza San Marco, Venice, c. 1909. (Above) Count Charles de Lambert circles the Eiffel Tower, 18 October 1909.

Eine Rundreise um die Türme. (Gegenüberliegende Seite) Das italienische Luftschiff *Parsival* ist am Campanile auf der Piazza San Marco befestigt, Venedig, um 1909. (Oben) Der Graf Charles de Lambert umkreist den Eiffelturm, 18. Oktober 1909.

Les plus hautes tours … (Page de gauche) Le dirigeable italien *Parsival* est amarré au Campanile de la Piazza San Marco, Venise, 1909. (Ci-dessus) Le comte Charles de Lambert fait le tour de la Tour Eiffel, 18 octobre 1909.

British royalty. Seated in the 12hp Panhard are (from left to right): Sir Charles Cust, royal equerry; Lord Llangattock and his son the Hon. C S Rolls (of Rolls-Royce); and the Duke of York (later George V). The date is 1900.

Britische Fürsten. In dem 12 PS starken Panhard sitzen (von links nach rechts): Sir Charles Cust, königlicher Stallmeister, Lord Llangattock und sein Sohn, der ehrenwerte C. S. Rolls (von Rolls-Royce), und der Herzog von York (der spätere George V.), 1900.

Altesses britanniques. Dans cette 12 CV Panhard sont assis (de gauche à droite) : Sir Charles Cust, écuyer royal ; Lord Llangattock et son fils l'honorable C. S. Rolls (celui des Rolls-Royce) ; enfin le duc d'York (futur George V). Nous sommes en 1900.

American aristocracy. Henry Ford lounges in the comfort of his
latest model, outside his own factory, c. 1905. The Model T and
assembly-line mass production were only three years away.

Amerikanischer Adel. Henry Ford sitzt sehr bequem in seinem
neuesten Modell vor der eigenen Fabrik, um 1905. Bis zum T-Modell
und zur Fließbandproduktion dauerte es nur noch drei Jahre.

Aristocratie américaine. Henry Ford se prélasse à l'intérieur de
son dernier modèle, devant son usine, vers 1905. On était à trois ans
de voir la première Ford T et la chaîne de production de masse.

A survivor from
an earlier age.
One of the last
penny farthing
cycles crosses
Hammersmith
Bridge, London,
1900.

Ein Überbleibsel
aus früheren Zeiten.
Mit einem der
letzten Hochräder
überquert ein Mann
die Hammersmith
Bridge, London,
1900.

Survivance de temps
ancien. L'un des
derniers bicycles
traversant le pont
de Hammersmith,
Londres, 1900.

Becoming acquainted. Her Ladyship gives one of her greys
a reassuring pat, 1904. These horses need not have worried –
they would have been kept on for ceremonial occasions.
For others, the knacker's yard beckoned.

Kurze Begrüßung. Ihre Ladyschaft gibt einem ihrer Schimmel
einen freundschaftlichen Klaps, 1904. Diese Pferde waren
nicht in Gefahr. Bei feierlichen Anlässen kamen sie weiterhin
zum Einsatz. Anderen drohte der Abdecker.

Les présentations. De son automobile, Madame flatte l'un de
ses chevaux d'une main rassurante, 1904. Cet attelage n'était
pas menacé, car on le gardait pour les grandes occasions.
Pour les autres chevaux, l'équarrisseur était là, qui attendait.

Alfred Hind Robinson's majestic panorama of the
Flying Scotsman heading north over the railway bridge
at Berwick-upon-Tweed, 29 May 1903. These were the
early days of the 'crack' expresses.

Das eindrucksvolle Panorama von Alfred Hind Robinson
vom *Flying Scotsman* auf der Fahrt nach Norden über
die Eisenbahnbrücke bei Berwick-upon-Tweed,
29. Mai 1903. Dies war der Beginn der „rasanten Zeit".

Un majestueux panorama d'Alfred Hind Robinson :
le *Flying Scotsman* s'engageant sur le pont de Berwick-
upon-Tweed pour foncer vers le nord, 29 mai 1903.
C'étaient les premiers jours des express « de tonnerre
et de feu ».

Crowds gather to
watch the fire brigade
deal with a derail-
ment on the Berlin
overhead railway,
September 1907.

Scharen strömen
zusammen, um der
Feuerwehr bei der
Bergung einer
entgleisten Berliner
Hochbahn zuzusehen,
September 1907.

On afflue pour
contempler la
brigade des pompiers
s'affairant après
le déraillement
d'un train sur le
pont de chemin de
fer de Berlin,
septembre 1907.

The tangled wreckage of the Zeppelin airship LZ 4 after it
caught fire at Echterdingen, 3 August 1908. The airship was the
fourth to be constructed by Count Ferdinand von Zeppelin.

Das verhedderte Wrack des Zeppelins LZ 4, nachdem es Feuer
gefangen hatte, Echterdingen, 3. August 1908. Es war das vierte
Luftschiff, das Graf Ferdinand von Zeppelin gebaut hatte.

Les débris enchevêtrés du zeppelin LZ 4 après qu'il eut brûlé à
Echterdingen, le 3 août 1908. Ce dirigeable était le quatrième
construit par le comte Ferdinand von Zeppelin.

The Brennan monorail has a day out, May 1907. The monorail was
designed by Louis Brennan, but initially many scoffed at its toy-like
appearance. (Above) Brennan's son negotiates a suspended cable.

Die Einschienenbahn von Brennan wird vorgestellt, Mai 1907.
Sie wurde von Louis Brennan entworfen. Anfangs spotteten viele
über die spielzeugartige Konstruktion. (Oben) Brennans Sohn fährt
über ein Schwebeseil.

Le monorail de Brennan est de sortie, mai 1907. Le monorail avait
été conçu par Louis Brennan, mais de par son aspect de jouet, il fut
tout d'abord l'objet de nombreuses moqueries. (Ci-dessus) Le fils
de Brennan se déplace sur un câble suspendu.

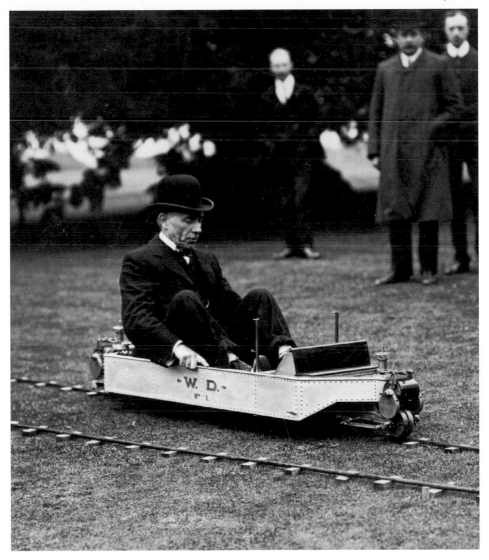

Bert Colver rides his 3.5hp Matchless at an Essex Motor Club
meeting, 8 August 1908. The motorcycle was the steed for the
new knight of the road – fast, reliable (sometimes), dangerous
and totally exhilarating.

Bert Colver fährt auf seiner 3,5 PS starken Matchless bei einem
Motorradclubtreffen in Essex, 8. August 1908. Das Motorrad
war das Ross der neuen Ritter der Straße – schnell, zuverlässig
(manchmal), gefährlich und sehr berauschend.

Bert Colver sur son 3,5 CV Matchless à une rencontre de
l'Essex Motor Club, 8 août 1908. Le motocycle était le
destrier des nouveaux chevaliers de la route : rapide, fiable
(parfois), dangereux et parfaitement grisant.

An early ancestor of the tanks of the First World War. Rustin and Hornby of Lincoln manufactured this caterpillar-track farm machine in 1902. The plough horse was about to join the cab horse in the ranks of the unemployed.

Ein früher Vorläufer der Panzerwagen des Ersten Weltkrieges. 1902 stellten Rustin und Hornby aus Lincoln dieses Raupenfahrzeug für die Landwirtschaft her. Das Pflugpferd stand kurz davor, in das Heer der arbeitslosen Omnibuspferde eingereiht zu werden.

Un ancêtre éloigné des tanks de la Première Guerre mondiale. Rustin et Hornby de Lincoln fabriquèrent cette machine agricole à chenille en 1902. Le cheval de trait était sur le point de rejoindre le cheval d'attelage dans les rangs des sans-emploi.

Henry Farman flies his
Voisin-Farman biplane over
1km, Issy-les-Moulineaux,
13 January 1908, and wins
the 50,000-franc Deutsch-
Archdeacon prize.

Henry Farman fliegt seinen
Voisin-Farman-Doppeldecker
über einen Kilometer weit,
Issy-les-Moulineaux,
13. Januar 1908. Er gewinnt
den mit 50 000 Francs dotier-
ten Deutsch-Archdeacon-Preis.

13 janvier 1908. Henry
Farman fait voler son biplan
Voisin-Farman sur 1 km à
Issy-les-Moulineaux et
remporte le prix Deutsch-
Archdeacon de 50 000 francs.

Overground luxury. The interior of the buffet saloon car on the
Great Western Railway, c. 1900. No expense was spared on the
fittings – plush upholstery, mahogany panelling, moulded ceilings.

Überirdischer Luxus. Die Inneneinrichtung des Speisewagens der
Great Western Railway, um 1900. Bei der Ausstattung wurden
keine Kosten gescheut – Plüschpolster, Mahagonivertäfelung und
gewölbte Decken.

Luxe de surface. L'intérieur du wagon-salon-buffet du Great
Western Railway, vers 1900. Aucune dépense n'était épargnée
pour des finitions impeccables : somptueux rembourrage,
panneaux d'acajou, moulures aux plafonds.

Underground functionalism. One of the passenger tunnels at Hampstead
Station on the newly-opened Northern Line extension of the London
Underground, 1909. The line connected the City with the wealthy suburbs
of north London.

Unterirdischer Funktionalismus. Einer der Fußgängertunnel der Station
Hampstead der neu eröffneten Nordlinienerweiterung der Londoner
Untergrundbahn, 1909. Diese Linie verband die Innenstadt mit den reichen
Vororten im Norden Londons.

Fonctionnalisme de sous-sol. L'un des tunnels réservés aux passagers, à la
station Hampstead de l'extension récente à la ligne Nord du métro londonien,
1909. La ligne reliait la City aux faubourgs résidentiels du nord de Londres.

13. Sport
Sport
Le sport

Goldsmith and Hewitt, in unlikely costume, exhibit illegal bare-knuckle skills in a carpeted room against a painted background, 1908. Even if the camera could not lie, it might attempt to deceive.

In merkwürdiger Kleidung zeigen Goldsmith und Hewitt verbotenerweise ihr Können mit bloßen Fäusten in einem mit Teppich ausgelegten Raum vor einem gemalten Hintergrund, 1908. Auch wenn die Kamera nicht lügen konnte, so schien sie hier doch einen Täuschungsversuch machen zu wollen.

Goldsmith et Hewitt, dans des costumes invraisemblables, exhibant illégalement leurs talents de lutteurs à main nue dans une pièce au sol recouvert d'un tapis, sur un fond peint, 1908. Si l'appareil photo ne pouvait mentir, il pouvait essayer de tromper.

13. Sport
Sport
Le sport

Never before had sport been so popular. Throughout the world crowds swarmed to stadiums, arenas, parks, clubs and race tracks. There were international matches and competitions in soccer, rugby, tennis, golf, athletics, motor racing and a dozen more manly (and, to an increasing degree, womanly) recreations. The first Davis Cup (tennis) tournament took place in 1900; the first Tour de France in 1903; the first rugby international between France and England and the first motor race at Le Mans in 1906.

Nations, states and cities competed with each other in newly-formed leagues and championships. To fans all over the world what mattered was 'victory'. When its local team won, a whole town celebrated. When a country lost, national pride suffered.

There were occasions when an entire race seemed bent on proving its superiority. In 1908 Jack Johnson became the first black boxer to be crowned World Heavyweight Champion. The hunt was immediately on to find the 'Great White Hope', a fighter capable of taking the title from Johnson. The man chosen was James J Jeffries, an ex-sparring partner of Gentleman Jim Corbett. Jeffries came out of retirement at the age of 35 to fight Johnson. But that fight came in the next decade...

Nie zuvor war Sport so beliebt gewesen. Überall auf der Welt strömten Menschenmengen in Stadien, Arenen, auf Sportplätze und Rennbahnen. Es gab internationale Begegnungen und Wettbewerbe im Fußball, Rugby, Tennis, Golf, bei der Leichtathletik, dem Rennsport und in vielen weiteren Männersportarten (und in einem immer stärkeren Maße auch bei den Frauen). Das erste Davis-Cup-Turnier (Tennis) wurde 1900, die erste Tour de France 1903 ausgetragen, das erste Rugbyländerspiel zwischen Frankreich und England und das erste Autorennen in Le Mans fanden 1906 statt.

Länder, Bundesstaaten und Städte konkurrierten mit ihren neuen Ligen und Meisterschaften. Was für Fans auf der ganzen Welt zählte, war der „Sieg". Gewann die Heimmannschaft, so feierte die ganze Stadt. Verlor aber ein Land, war der Stolz der ganzen Nation getroffen.

Es gab Anlässe, bei denen ein Wettkampf darauf angelegt schien, die Überlegenheit der einen oder anderen Hautfarbe zu beweisen. 1908 wurde Jack Johnson als erster schwarzer Boxer Weltmeister im Schwergewicht. Sofort fing die Suche nach der „großen weißen Hoffnung" an, nach einem Boxer, der Johnson den Titel abnehmen sollte. Der Auserwählte war James J. Jeffries, ein ehemaliger Sparringspartner von Gentleman Jim Corbett. Jeffries hatte bereits mit dem Boxen aufgehört, kämpfte aber doch noch einmal im Alter von 35 Jahren gegen Johnson. Dieser Kampf sollte jedoch erst ein Jahrzehnt später stattfinden …

Le sport n'avait jamais été aussi populaire. Partout dans le monde, les foules affluaient dans les stades, les arènes, les parcs, les clubs et les champs de courses. Il y avait des matches et des compétitions internationales de football, rugby, tennis, golf, athlétisme, courses de voitures et une douzaines d'autres disciplines masculines et, de plus en plus, féminines. Le premier tournoi de la coupe Davis (tennis) se déroula en 1900 ; le premier Tour de France en 1903 ; le premier international de rugby entre la France et l'Angleterre en 1906, la même année que la première course automobile du Mans.

Les pays et les villes entraient en compétition par l'entremise de ligues et de championnats nouvellement créés. Pour les supporters du monde entier, l'important était la « victoire ». Des villes entières étaient en fête quand leur équipe locale gagnait un match. Quand un pays perdait, la fierté nationale en souffrait.

Il arrivait que tout un groupe s'efforçât de prouver sa supériorité. En 1908, Jack Johnson devint le premier boxeur noir champion du monde des poids lourds. On se mit alors à la recherche du prochain « grand espoir blanc », capable de prendre son titre à Johnson. L'homme choisi fut James J. Jeffries. Ce dernier sortit de sa retraite à l'âge de 35 ans pour combattre contre Johnson. Mais le combat n'eut lieu qu'à la décennie suivante …

Pat Ewry of the United States practises for the standing high jump at the London Olympic Games, 1 July 1908. In the Games themselves, Ewry won gold medals for this event, the standing long jump and the standing triple jump.

Pat Ewry aus den Vereinigten Staaten übt für den Hochsprung aus dem Stand bei den Olympischen Spielen in London, 1. Juli 1908. Bei den Spielen selbst gewann Ewry Goldmedaillen in dieser Disziplin, im Weitsprung und im Dreisprung aus dem Stand.

L'Américain Pat Ewry s'exerçant au saut en hauteur à pieds joints aux Jeux olympiques de Londres, 1ᵉʳ juillet 1908. À ces Jeux, Ewry remporta des médailles d'or pour cette épreuve ainsi que pour le saut en longueur à pieds joints et le triple saut à pieds joints.

Alfred Shrubb of
Great Britain, one
of the best long
distance runners
of the early 20th
century, c. 1909.

Alfred Shrubb aus
Großbritannien,
einer der besten
Langstreckenläufer
Anfang des 20. Jahr-
hunderts, um 1909.

Le Britannique
Alfred Shrubb,
l'un des meilleurs
coureurs de fond du
début du XXᵉ siècle,
vers 1909.

John Taylor of the United States poses for a press camera in front of
the empty seats of the White City Stadium, July 1908. Taylor was
competing in the quarter mile event at the London Olympics.

John Taylor aus den Vereinigten Staaten, fotografiert von einem
Pressefotografen vor der leeren Zuschauertribüne des White City
Stadium, Juli 1908. Taylor nahm in der Disziplin des 400-Meter-
Laufs bei den Olympischen Spielen in London teil.

L'Américain John Taylor posant pour la presse devant les sièges vides
du stade de White City, juillet 1908. Taylor était l'un des concurrents
de l'épreuve du quart de mile aux Jeux olympiques de Londres.

One of the team of
Danish women
gymnasts limbers up
for the London
Olympics, July 1908.
It was an event the
Danes dominated.

Eine Turnerin aus
dem dänischen
Frauenteam wärmt
sich bei den Olympi-
schen Spielen in
London auf, Juli
1908. In dieser
Disziplin führten
die Däninnen.

L'un des membres de
l'équipe danoise de
gymnastique à
l'échauffement aux
Jeux olympiques de
Londres, juillet
1908. Les Danoises
dominaient dans
cette épreuve.

Canadian Robert Carr
(extreme right) wins the final
of the 100-yard sprint at the
British Amateur Athletic
Association Championships
at the White City, London,
July 1908. Second was
Robert Walker of South
Africa (third from right).

Der Kanadier Robert Carr
(ganz rechts) gewinnt im
Finale des 100-Meter-Laufs
bei den britischen Leicht
athletikmeisterschaften des
Amateurverbands (Amateur
Athletic Association Cham-
pionships) im White City
Stadium, London, Juli 1908.
Zweiter wurde Robert
Walker aus Südafrika (Dritter
von rechts).

Le Canadien Robert Carr
(à l'extrême droite) remporte
la finale du 100 mètres aux
championnats de l'Association britannique d'athlétisme
en amateur à White City,
Londres, juillet 1908.
Le second était le Sud-
Africain Robert Walker
(troisième à partir de
la droite).

Not the last cavalry charge in British history, but a disastrous moment as jockeys and mounts come down to earth in the Grand National at Aintree racecourse, Liverpool.

Dies ist nicht der letzte Sturmangriff der Kavallerie in der britischen Geschichte, sondern ein furchtbarer Augenblick, als Jockeys und Pferde beim Grand National auf der Aintree-Rennbahn, Liverpool, zu Boden gehen.

Il ne s'agit pas de la dernière charge de cavalerie dans l'histoire britannique, mais bien du moment désastreux où les jockeys et leurs montures entrèrent en collision et tombèrent à terre, lors du Grand National du champ de course d'Aintree, Liverpool.

The Sport of Kings, but apparently not of gentlemen. The English
upper classes enjoy a day at the races, while a young woman hugs
her feather boa and waits for attention. And all this at Ascot!

Die Disziplin der Könige, doch anscheinend nicht die der Kavaliere.
Die englische Oberschicht genießt einen Renntag. Währenddessen
hält sich eine junge Frau an ihrer Federboa fest und wartet auf
Aufmerksamkeit. Und das beim Pferderennen in Ascot!

Le sport des rois, mais sûrement pas celui des gentlemen !
Des membres de l'aristocratie anglaise suivent la course, tandis
qu'une jeune femme tenant serré son boa attend qu'on lui accorde
un peu d'attention. Et tout ça à Ascot !

Another section of the crowd at Ascot on 1 June 1907. Ascot was the most important race meeting on the social calendar. One simply had to be seen there, looking one's best and hobnobbing with all the right people.

Weitere Zuschauer in Ascot am 1. Juni 1907. Ascot galt in Bezug auf Pferderennen als wichtigster Termin für die Gesellschaft. Hier musste man einfach gesehen werden, blendend aussehen und mit allen wichtigen Leuten plaudern.

À Ascot toujours, le 1ᵉʳ juin 1907. La course de chevaux d'Ascot était la réunion la plus importante sur le calendrier mondain. Il suffisait de s'y montrer habillé le mieux possible en compagnie des gens en vue.

Alfred Trott of Middlesex County Cricket Club bowling on a
practice ground. Trott was also a batsman of considerable talent,
and is the only cricketer to have hit a ball over the Pavilion at Lord's.

Alfred Trott vom Middlesex County Cricket Club beim Werfen auf
dem Übungsplatz. Trott war auch ein besonders talentierter
Schlagmann. Er ist der einzige Kricketspieler, der einen Ball über
den Pavillon auf dem Lord's Cricket Ground geschlagen hat.

Alfred Trott, du Middlesex County Cricket Club, lançant la balle sur
un terrain d'entraînement. Trott était également un batteur (cricket)
de premier rang et le seul joueur à avoir réussi à lancer une balle
par-dessus le pavillon du terrain de Lord.

The Father of
Modern Cricket.
Dr William Gilbert
Grace was still in his
prime when this
photograph was
taken in 1900.

Der Vater des
modernen Kricket-
spiels. Dr. William
Gilbert Grace war
auf dem Höhepunkt
seiner Karriere,
als dieses Foto im
Jahre 1900 aufge-
nommen wurde.

Le père du
cricket moderne.
Le Dr. William
Gilbert Grace était
à l'apogée de son
art lorsque cette
photo fut prise,
en 1900.

The trophy table at the Richmond Horse Show, 14 June 1907.
Then, as now, Richmond was always a most law-abiding place,
and the policeman on guard is clearly bored out of his skull.

Der Pokaltisch bei der Pferdeschau in Richmond,
14. Juni 1907. Noch heute ist Richmond eine sehr gesetzes-
treue Gemeinde. Der diensthabende Polizist ist offensichtlich
ziemlich gelangweilt.

La table des trophées au Richmond Horse Show,
14 juin 1907. Alors comme aujourd'hui, Richmond était un
lieu respectueux des lois et ce policier de garde est visiblement
mort d'ennui.

In the days before indecipherable public address systems, spectators relied on the inaudible voice of the City toastmaster to keep them up to date with what was happening at the London Olympics of 1908.

Bevor es schlecht verständliche Lautsprecheranlagen gab, vertrauten die Zuschauer auf die kaum hörbaren Worte des Stadionsprechers. Dieser hielt sie bei den Olympischen Spielen in London 1908 auf dem aktuellen Stand des Geschehens.

En ces temps d'avant les sytèmes d'affichage digital, les spectateurs devaient s'en remettre à la voix à peine audible d'un maître de cérémonie pour être tenus au courant du déroulement des Jeux olympiques de 1908.

The man who came second but won the gold medal: John Hayes of the USA completes the Olympic marathon, 24 July 1908.

Dieser Mann erreichte als Zweiter das Ziel und gewann dennoch die Goldmedaille. John Hayes aus den USA beim Zieleinlauf des olympischen Marathonlaufs, 24. Juli 1908.

L'homme qui arriva second mais remporta la médaille d'or : l'Américain John Hayes termine le marathon olympique, 24 juillet 1908.

Triumph to tragedy. Dorando Pietri of Italy is helped across the finishing line in the same marathon and is subsequently disqualified. He had entered the stadium well ahead of Hayes, but in his confused exhaustion had turned the wrong way. His assistant in the tweeds is the writer Sir Arthur Conan Doyle.

Ein folgenschwerer Sieg. Im selben Marathonlauf hilft man Dorando Pietri aus Italien über die Ziellinie. Im Nachhinein wird er disqualifiziert. Er war weit vor Hayes ins Stadion eingelaufen, doch in seiner Erschöpfung und Verwirrung lief er in die falsche Richtung. Sein Ratgeber im Tweedanzug ist der Schriftsteller Sir Arthur Conan Doyle.

Du triomphe à la tragédie. L'Italien Dorando Pietri, aidé à passer la ligne dans le même marathon, est disqualifié. Il était entré dans le stade bien devant Hayes, mais dans la confusion due à l'épuisement, avait pris un mauvais tournant. Son assistant en costume de tweed est l'écrivain Sir Arthur Conan Doyle.

Bob Fitzsimmons, c.1900. Fitzsimmons was the first fighter to win three world titles – middleweight (1891), heavyweight (1897) and light-heavyweight (1903).

Bob Fitzsimmons, um 1900. Fitzsimmons war der erste Boxer, der drei Weltmeistertitel gewann – im Mittelgewicht (1891), Schwergewicht (1897) und Halbschwergewicht (1903).

Bob Fitzsimmons, vers 1900. Fitzsimmons fut le premier boxeur à remporter trois titres mondiaux : poids moyens (1891), poids lourds (1897) et milourds (1903).

Reinhold Thiele's
portrait of the
American boxer
James J Jeffries,
c. 1900. Jeffries had
taken the world
heavyweight title
from Fitzsimmons
a year earlier.

Ein Porträt des ame-
rikanischen Boxers
James J. Jeffries von
Reinhold Thiele,
um 1900. Ein Jahr
zuvor hatte Jeffries
Fitzsimmons den
Weltmeistertitel im
Schwergewicht
abgenommen.

Portrait par
Reinhold Thiele du
boxeur américain
James J. Jeffries, vers
1900. L'année précé-
dente, Jeffries avait
pris à Fitzsimmons
le titre mondial
des poids lourds.

Sumo wrestlers in action, 1909. Following the heroic Japanese victory in the
war against Russia, there was a craze in the West for all things Japanese –
furniture, music, costume, decoration and martial arts. And sumo? Who knows?

Sumoringer beim Kampf, 1909. Nach dem heldenhaften Sieg Japans im Krieg
gegen Russland war man im Westen verrückt nach allem, was japanisch war –
Möbel, Musik, Mode, Einrichtungsgegenstände und asiatische Kampfsportarten.
Auch nach Sumo? Wer weiß das schon?

Des lutteurs de sumo en pleine action, 1909. Après l'héroïque victoire japonaise
contre la Russie, l'Occident s'engoua de tout ce qui venait du Japon :
meubles, musique, vêtements, décorations et arts martiaux. Et le sumo ? Hmm …

Time-out from the playing fields of Eton, c. 1900. The Eton
soccer team psyching itself up before an important game.
One hopes that they calmed down before play started.

Auszeit am Rande des Spielfelds von Eton, um 1900.
Die Fußballmannschaft von Eton bereitet sich auf ein wichtiges
Spiel vor. Hoffentlich beruhigten sie sich noch vor Spielbeginn.

Temps mort sur le terrain de sport d'Eton, vers 1900.
L'équipe de football d'Eton cherchant l'inspiration avant un jeu
important. On espère qu'ils parvinrent à trouver le calme avant
le début du match …

A women's volleyball game, 1900. The setting is almost certainly a college somewhere in the United States.

Frauen spielen Volleyball, 1900. Schauplatz ist wahrscheinlich ein College irgendwo in den Vereinigten Staaten.

Un match féminin de volley-ball, 1900. La scène se déroule probablement dans un college quelque part aux États-Unis.

A smoky start to
the Indianapolis
100-Mile Race at the
Speedway, c. 1909.
By this time cars
were capable
of 100mph.

Viel Qualm
beim Start zum
100-Meilen-Rennen
auf dem Indianapolis
Speedway, um 1909.
Zu dieser Zeit
konnten Autos
schon 160 km/h
schnell fahren.

Un nuage de fumée
marque le départ
de cette course
(100 miles) sur le
circuit d'Indiana-
polis, vers 1909.
À cette époque,
les voitures de
course atteignaient
160 km/h.

Body puncher. Frederick Grace, the British lightweight boxer who won the Olympic gold medal in London in the summer of 1908.

Der Boxer Frederick Grace. Das britische Leicht-gewicht gewann Olympisches Gold in London im Sommer 1908.

Un gars qui a du punch. Frederick Grace, le poids léger britannique qui remporta la médaille d'or olympique à Londres, l'été 1908.

Body builder.
Reinhold Thiele's
portrait of
Mr Murray,
proud winner of
the Sandow body-
building competi-
tion, 1905.

Bodybuilder.
Reinhold Thieles
Porträt von
Herrn Murray, dem
stolzen Gewinner
im Bodybuilding-
wettkampf von
Sandow, 1905.

Un gars qui a du
coffre. Portrait par
Reinhold Thiele de
Mr Murray, fier
champion de la
compétition de
body-building de
Sandow, 1905.

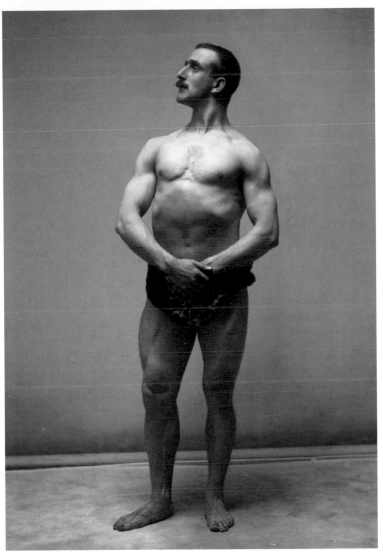

14. Children
Kinder
Les enfants

The street could be almost anywhere in the Western world.
The clothes and the boots that the little girl is wearing are those
of 1905. But the smile is universal and eternal.

Diese Straße könnte sich fast überall in der westlichen Welt befinden.
Die Kleidung und die Schuhe, die das kleine Mädchen trägt, stammen
aus dem Jahre 1905. Aber das Lächeln ist zeit- und grenzenlos.

Cette photo pourrait avoir été prise n'importe où dans le monde
occidental. Les vêtements et les bottines que porte cette petite fille sont
de 1905. Mais son sourire est universel et éternel.

14. Children
Kinder
Les enfants

Slowly but steadily, life was becoming more comfortable for the very young, though poverty or a cruel Nanny could still bring infant misery. Children ceased to be 'little adults' and gained lives of their own. There were charities and foundations to protect children, to cater for their needs, to rescue them from the worst of plights. Psychologists claimed it was possible to understand the minds of children. At the Sorbonne, Alfred Binet believed he had even found a way of measuring their intelligence.

But children still posed problems for society. Discipline was rigorously imposed by passing adults. Few days passed in any school without the swish of the cane in every classroom. Policeman had no hesitation in boxing the ears of window breakers, apple scrumpers or any other 'little devils'.

During those rare times when children escaped from the adult world, they collected birds' eggs, fished for tiddlers, dammed streams, fought each other, got lost, were by turn kind and cruel to animals, and failed to take care of their clothes. It is to be hoped that they had fun, for a chain of events was already in progress that would viciously cut short the adult lives of millions of them in the next decade.

Langsam, aber stetig verbesserte sich das Leben der Kleinen, obwohl Armut oder ein grausames Kindermädchen den Kindern immer noch Kummer und Leid bereiten konnten. Die Kinder hörten auf, „kleine Erwachsene" zu sein und hatten eine Kindheit. Es gab Wohlfahrtseinrichtungen und Stiftungen, die die Kinder unter ihre Fittiche nahmen, sie mit Essen versorgten und sie vor Unglück bewahrten. Psychologen waren der Meinung, dass es möglich war, die Gemüter der Kinder zu verstehen. Alfred Binet von der Sorbonne glaubte, dass er einen Weg gefunden hatte, die Intelligenz der Kinder zu messen.

Nach wie vor wurden Kinder jedoch als störend empfunden. Erwachsene Passanten sorgten für strengen Gehorsam. In den Schulen und Klassenräumen gab es nur wenige Tage, an denen nicht der Rohrstock niedersauste. Auch die Polizisten zögerten nicht, den Kindern eine Ohrfeige zu verpassen, wenn sie Fensterscheiben eingeworfen, Äpfel geklaut oder anderen Unfug getrieben hatten.

In den seltenen Fällen, in denen die Kinder der Welt der Erwachsenen entkommen konnten, gingen sie Vogeleier sammeln, kleine Fische fangen, bauten Dämme in kleinen Flüsschen, balgten und verirrten sich. Sie waren lieb und grausam zugleich zu Tieren und gaben nicht auf ihre Kleidung Acht. Hoffen wir, dass sie Spaß hatten. Denn eine Reihe von Ereignissen war bereits im Gange, die im nächsten Jahrzehnt auf schreckliche Weise das Leben vieler von ihnen verkürzen sollte.

La vie devenait plus facile pour les plus petits, même si la pauvreté ou une méchante nurse pouvaient encore les rendre malheureux. Les enfants n'étaient plus considérés comme de « petits adultes », mais avaient le droit de grandir. Il existait des institutions de charité et des fondations de protection de l'enfance qui pourvoyaient à leurs besoins et les secouraient dans leur détresse. Les psychologues affirmaient que l'on pouvait comprendre l'esprit d'un enfant. Alfred Binet croyait même avoir trouvé un moyen de mesurer leur intelligence.

Mais les enfants posaient toujours des problèmes à la société. Une discipline rigoureuse était imposée par des adultes de passage. Peu de jours s'écoulaient dans les écoles sans le sifflement du fouet dans toutes les classes. La police n'hésitait pas à chauffer les oreilles des briseurs de vitres, des voleurs de pommes ou d'autres « petits diables ».

Dans les rares moments où les enfants parvenaient à s'échapper du monde des adultes, ils ramassaient des œufs d'oiseaux, se délectaient de parties de pêches, construisaient des barrages, se bagarraient entre eux, se perdaient, cajolaient ou torturaient les animaux et prenaient peu de soin de leurs vêtements. On espère qu'ils s'amusaient beaucoup, car les événements qui allaient couper net le fil des vies de millions d'entre eux s'enchaînaient déjà.

Water gypsies. It may have been an exceptionally warm autumn day or the water may have looked especially inviting. Paul Martin's photograph shows a group of lads getting dressed after a swim in the Serpentine, Hyde Park, London, October 1900.

Große Wasserratten. Vielleicht war es ein besonders warmer Herbsttag, oder das Wasser sah besonders einladend aus. Die Aufnahme von Paul Martin zeigt eine Gruppe von Jungen, die sich nach dem Schwimmen im Serpentine wieder anziehen, Hyde Park, London, Oktober 1900.

Gamins d'eau douce. Peut-être était-ce un jour d'automne exceptionnellement chaud, ou l'eau semblait-elle particulièrement invitante … Cette photo de Paul Martin montre un groupe de jeunes garçons se rhabillant après une partie de natation dans la Serpentine, Hyde Park, Londres, octobre 1900.

Water babies. Doting, and hopefully strong, parents, give their children a swimming lesson in the River Thames at Wallingford, September 1906. Upstream, the Thames was relatively free from pollution.

Kleine Wasserratten. Eltern, die in ihre Kinder vernarrt und hoffentlich stark genug waren, geben ihren Kleinen Schwimmunterricht in der Themse bei Wallingford, September 1906. Stromaufwärts war die Themse relativ sauber.

Bébés d'eau douce. Des parents aimants et, on l'espère, aux bras solides, donnent une leçon de natation à leurs enfants dans la Tamise à Wallingford, septembre 1906. Dans sa partie amont, l'eau de la Tamise était relativement propre.

The children's playground on the roof of the Ellis Island Immigration
Centre, New York, c. 1905. The sides of the wagon are inscribed with
the words 'Uncle Sam'. A new patriotism was already taking over.

Der Kinderspielplatz auf dem Dach des Ellis Island Immigration Centre,
New York, um 1905. Auf den Seiten des kleinen Wagens stehen die
Worte „Uncle Sam". Eine neue Vaterlandsliebe kam bereits wieder auf.

Le terrain de jeux des enfants sur le toit du Centre d'immigration d'Ellis
Island, New York, vers 1905. Sur le côté de la petite voiture, sont inscrits
les mots « Oncle Sam ». Un nouveau patriotisme prenait le dessus.

The massed ranks
of the Esperance
Society Morris
Dance Group
arrives at Cumber-
land Market,
May Day 1909.

Die Truppe der
Esperance Society
Morris Dance
Group bei ihrer
Ankunft auf dem
Cumberland Markt,
1. Mai 1909.

En rangs serrés,
les petits danseurs
du Groupe Morris
de la Société Espé-
rance débarquent
au marché de
Cumberland,
le 1ᵉʳ mai 1909.

Boy Scouts at a camp in 1908. It was the year that Robert Baden-Powell founded the Scout movement and published *Scouting for Boys*. Six years later most of these boys would probably undergo more rigorous training.

Pfadfinder auf einem Lagerplatz im Jahre 1908. In diesem Jahr gründete Robert Baden-Powell die Pfadfinderbewegung und veröffentlichte das Buch *Scouting for Boys*. Sechs Jahre später wurden viele dieser Jungen wahrscheinlich härteren Übungen unterzogen.

Un camp de scouts en 1908. Cette année-là, Baden-Powell fonda le mouvement scout et publia son livre, *Scouting for Boys*. Six ans plus tard, la plupart de ces garçons auraient sans doute à subir un entraînement bien plus rigoureux.

A choir of angels – it is to be hoped. Choristers selected to sing at the Coronation of King Edward VII pose for the camera outside the Chapel Royal, St James's, London, June 1902.

Ein Engelschor – so sollte man jedenfalls annehmen. Ausgewählte Chorknaben sollen bei der Krönungsfeier von König Edward VII. singen und posieren hier für ein Foto vor der königlichen St. James Kapelle, London, Juni 1902.

Un chœur d'anges – on l'espère. Les enfants de chœur choisis pour chanter lors du couronnement du roi Édouard VII posent pour la photo devant la chapelle royale, Saint James, Londres, juin 1902.

The one that didn't get away. London children admire
the catch of the day – a small gudgeon, 1905. Lakes in the
London parks were open to young anglers a hundred
years ago.

Der Eine, der nicht entkam. Londoner Kinder bestaunen
den Fang des Tages – einen kleinen Gründling, 1905.
Vor 100 Jahren durften die kleinen Angler in den kleinen
Seen der Londoner Parks fischen.

La prise. Des gamins de Londres admirent la prise du jour,
un petit goujon, 1905. Il y a cent ans, les lacs des parcs
londoniens étaient tous accessibles aux petits pêcheurs.

The one that couldn't get away. The annual scramble for a piece of the
Lenten Pancake at Westminster School, 1905. Traditionally, the chef
tossed the pancake over a bar in the School Hall, and then scholars fought
for the bits.

Einer, der nicht entkommen konnte. Die jährliche Balgerei um ein Stück
vom Eierkuchen am Fastnachtsdienstag an der Westminster School, 1905.
Nach der Tradition warf der Koch den Eierkuchen in die Schulhalle.
Daraufhin kämpften die Schüler um die Kuchenstücke.

La ruée. La mêlée rituelle autour de la galette de carême à Westminster
School, 1905. La tradition voulait que le cuisinier lançât la crêpe par-dessus
une barre dans la Grande salle ; les étudiants s'arrachaient alors les morceaux.

Working lads. Three pit boys from Newcastle, in the north of
England, 1909. School attendance was compulsory only up to the age
of twelve. From then on, most boys and girls looked to earn a living.

Arbeiterjungen. Drei Zechenjungen aus Newcastle, im Norden
von England, 1909. Schulpflichtig war man damals nur bis zum
12. Lebensjahr. Danach sahen die meisten Jungen und Mädchen zu,
dass sie sich ihren Lebensunterhalt verdienten.

Des gamins au travail. Trois petits mineurs dans le nord de
l'Angleterre, 1909. L'école était obligatoire jusqu'à 12 ans seulement.
Ensuite, la plupart des garçons et des filles devaient travailler pour
gagner leur vie.

Watching lasses. A largely female crowd gathers to watch a Punch and Judy Show, 1905. The children are smartly dressed. Either this was a special occasion or it was a prosperous neighbourhood.

Mädchenaugen. Eine große Zuschauermenge kleiner Mädchen ist hier versammelt, um sich ein Kasperletheater anzusehen, 1905. Die Kinder sind herausgeputzt, was darauf hindeutet, dass dies entweder ein besonderer Anlass oder eine reiche Gegend war.

Des fillettes au spectacle. Une foule très majoritairement féminine assemblée pour voir un spectacle de marionnettes, 1905. Ces petites filles sont bien habillées : on peut alors supposer qu'il s'agit d'une sortie exceptionnelle ou bien que nous nous trouvons dans un quartier prospère.

In the footsteps
of Sitting Bull.
The Indian wars
were long over, and
only cameras were
aimed at this young
Sioux brave in 1907.

In den Fußstapfen
von Sitting Bull.
Die Indianerkriege
waren längst vor-
über. Hier zielten
nur Kameras auf
diesen kleinen,
mutigen Sioux
im Jahre 1907.

Sur les pas de
Sitting Bull. Les
guerres indiennes
étaient finies depuis
longtemps et seul
un appareil photo
pouvait « viser »
ce jeune brave
sioux en 1907.

In the footsteps
of Little Lord
Fauntleroy.
Master Prixley
enjoys his comic,
28 July 1903.

In den Fußstapfen
des Kleinen Lords
Fauntleroy. Der
Junge Prixley hat
Freude am Lesen
seines Bilderbuchs,
28. Juli 1903.

Sur les pas du petit
Lord Fauntleroy.
Le sieur Prixley lit
son journal illustré,
28 juillet 1903.

A lesson in oral hygiene, 1908. The slogan on the blackboard reads 'Spare the brush and spoil the TEETH'. Few people maintained a full set of teeth into adulthood at this time and most had a fear of dentistry.

Zahnputzstunde, 1908. Auf der Tafel steht „Schonst du die Bürste, verdirbst du die ZÄHNE". Zu dieser Zeit behielten nur wenige Leute all ihre Zähne, bis sie erwachsen waren, und die meisten hatten Angst vor dem Zahnarzt.

Leçon d'hygiène buccale, 1908. Le slogan au tableau noir dit : « Ménager sa brosse à dents, c'est abîmer ses DENTS ». À l'époque, arrivés à l'âge adulte, peu de gens avaient encore toutes leurs dents ; la plupart avaient une peur bleue du dentiste.

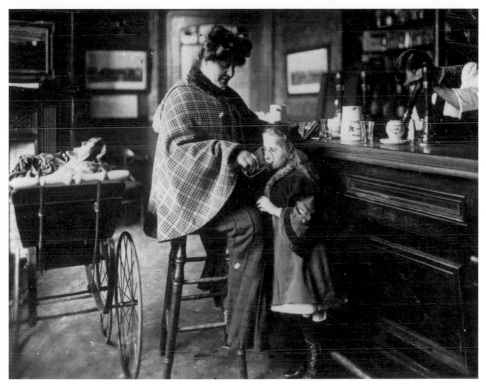

Never too young to learn. A mother gives her daughter a drop of the hard stuff at the bar of a public house, 1900. Licensing laws were less stringent at this time. Pubs stayed open all day and children were admitted.

Man ist nie zu jung zum Lernen. Eine Mutter gibt ihrer Tochter einen Tropfen „Hartes" an der Bar einer Kneipe, 1900. Die Schankkonzessionen waren damals nicht so streng. Die Kneipen waren den ganzen Tag geöffnet und Kinder hatten Zutritt.

On n'est jamais trop jeune pour apprendre. Une mère fait goûter de l'alcool à sa fille au bar d'un pub, 1900. Les licences de débits de boissons étaient moins strictes qu'aujourd'hui. Les pubs restaient ouverts toute la journée et les enfants y étaient admis.

There was little to keep children at home after school or on Sundays. They roamed the streets, seeking excitement. With luck they might find an ice-cream stall (opposite) or a game at the Chelsea Bridge Road Fair (above).

Nach der Schule oder an Sonntagen konnte man die Kinder nur schwer im Hause halten. Sie streiften in den Straßen umher auf der Suche nach Abenteuern. Wenn sie Glück hatten, fanden sie einen Eisstand (gegenüberliegende Seite) oder irgendeinen anderen Zeitvertreib bei der Chelsea Bridge Road Fair (oben).

Peu de choses pouvaient retenir les enfants à la maison après l'école ou les dimanches. Ils vagabondaient dans les rues à la recherche de distractions. Avec un peu de chance, ils tombaient sur une marchande de glace (ci-contre) ou sur un jeu à la foire de Chelsea Bridge Road (ci-dessus).

A generation earlier, children born with a handicap (the word was used freely then) received little special training or education. Here, blind boys from the Royal Normal College, Upper Norwood, London, perform on the parallel bars, July 1907.

Noch eine Generation zuvor hatten Kinder, die mit einer Behinderung (das Wort wurde ungeniert benutzt) zur Welt gekommen waren, kaum ein besonderes Training oder eine spezielle Ausbildung erhalten. Hier sieht man blinde Jungen vom Royal Normal College, Upper Norwood, London. Sie zeigen ihr Können am Barren, Juli 1907.

Une génération plus tôt, les enfants nés avec un handicap (ce terme était alors utilisé sans gêne) ne recevaient pas d'enseignement spécial ou adapté. Ici, des garçons malvoyants du Royal Normal College, Upper Norwood, Londres, exécutent des figures aux barres parallèles, juillet 1907.

A writing class at the Oral Deaf and Dumb Institute, Fitzroy Square, London, 8 May 1908. Provision was erratic, and there was generally less help available in country districts.

Eine Schreibstunde in einer Taubstummenanstalt, Fitzroy Square, London, 8. Mai 1908. Der Unterricht fand nicht regelmäßig statt. Im Allgemeinen gab es auf dem Lande nur wenig Unterstützung in dieser Hinsicht.

Une classe d'écriture à l'Institut des sourds et muets, Fitzroy Square, Londres, 8 mai 1908. Les cours étaient erratiques et il y avait généralement encore moins de prise en charge dans les régions rurales.

Oh, the joys of drill in the schoolyard, 1906. And the steely eye of the teacher could spot any slacker among the 200 or so on parade.

Oje, der geliebte Frühsport auf dem Schulhof, 1906. Der Lehrer konnte mit seinem strengen und scharfen Blick jeden Faulpelz in der Truppe der 200 Kinder ausfindig machen.

Ah, les joies de l'exercice dans la cour de l'école ! Et l'œil acéré du maître, capable de repérer immédiatement le fainéant parmi les 200 élèves à la parade, 1906.

15. All human life
Menschliches, Allzumenschliches
Les petits et les grands événements de la vie

The English take to the *piste*. A beginner sets out on the lower
slopes of (a rather flat) Northamptonshire, December 1908.
Her Edwardian clothing did little to help her in her struggles.

Die Engländer fangen mit dem Skilaufen an. Eine Anfängerin macht
sich auf den Weg zu einem flacheren Abhang im (ziemlich flachen),
Northamptonshire, Dezember 1908. Ihre Kleidung aus der Zeit
Edwards VII. war ihr bei ihren Bemühungen nicht gerade hilfreich.

Les Anglais prennent la piste. Une skieuse débutante s'engage sur
les flancs peu abrupts (et même plutôt plats) du Northamptonshire,
décembre 1908. La mode édouardienne n'était pas faite pour faciliter
ses efforts.

15. All human life
Menschliches, Allzumenschliches
Les petits et les grands événements de la vie

New hopes, dreams, inventions and ideas brought a clutch of innovative eccentricities to a new century. The seriously deranged gave themselves shocks, endangered their lungs, challenged buses and lorries to tug-of-war contests, and flew their fluttering biplanes as close to the ground as possible – or even closer. The truly mad killed themselves in any number of imaginative ways.

Intrepid adventurers trudged further south or north than anyone had previously ventured. Everything and everywhere in the 1900s was the 'greatest' – the tallest, longest, newest, fastest, highest, lowest and often stupidest. Science thrilled amateurs and professionals alike, and its seemingly magic qualities delighted many. The world shrank. Whereas it had taken weeks for Britain to learn of the Indian Mutiny 50 years earlier, news could now cross the globe in a matter of minutes. East met west in unlikely places on unlikely occasions. People laughed and cried, danced and sang, lifted their spirits, sank into depression (a relatively new concept), loved and loathed, shrugged off the past and hastened to what they believed was a bright new future. Another decade came and went.

Neue Hoffnungen, Träume, Erfindungen und Ideen brachten im neuen Jahrhundert eine Fülle von ausgefallenen Neuheiten hervor. Exzentrische Erfinder gaben sich Elektroschocks, gefährdeten ihre Lungen, forderten Busse und Lastautos zu einem Tauziehen heraus und flogen mit ihren klapprigen Doppeldeckern so tief wie nur irgend möglich am Boden entlang – manchmal sogar noch tiefer. Die Fanatiker unter ihnen kamen bei diesen Versuchen auf die wundersamsten Arten und Weisen ums Leben.

Abenteurer stapften südlicher und nördlicher als es jemals zuvor jemand gewagt hatte. Man maß jede Sache und jeden Ort in Superlativen – das Höchste, Längste, Neuste,

Schnellste, Größte, Niedrigste und oft das Dümmste. Die Wissenschaft begeisterte Laien und Profis gleichermaßen. Viele erfreuten sich an ihrer scheinbar magischen Fähigkeit. Die Welt schrumpfte zusammen. Während es 50 Jahre zuvor noch Wochen dauerte, bis Großbritannien von dem Aufstand in Indien erfuhr, konnten Nachrichten nun innerhalb von wenigen Minuten rund um den Globus geschickt werden. Der Osten traf an den unterschiedlichsten Orten und zu unterschiedlichsten Anlässen auf die westliche Zivilisation. Die Menschen lachten und weinten, tanzten und sangen, hatten geistige Höhenflüge, bekamen Depressionen (damals ein relativ neuer Begriff), liebten und hassten. Sie taten die Vergangenheit mit einem Achselzucken ab und eilten auf die – ihrer Ansicht nach – neue glänzende Zukunft zu. Ein anderes Jahrzehnt kam und ging vorüber.

Nouveaux espoirs, rêves, inventions et idées amenèrent tout un sillage d'innovations plus ou moins excentriques. Les insensés se faisaient des frayeurs, mettaient leurs poumons en dangers, lançaient des défis guerriers aux autobus et aux camions et faisaient voler leurs palpitants bi-plans au ras du sol – et parfois plus bas encore. Les fous authentiques se tuaient de toutes sortes de manières avec parfois beaucoup d'imagination.

D'intrépides aventuriers gagnaient péniblement des points, à l'extrême sud ou à l'extrême nord, plus loin que personne avant eux n'avait osé le faire. Dans les années 1900, tout et tous les lieux étaient « le plus » : le plus grand, le plus long, le plus nouveau, le plus rapide, le plus haut, le plus bas et, souvent, le plus stupide. La science tournait la tête aux amateurs comme aux spécialistes et ses aspects faussement magiques en ravissaient plus d'un. Le monde rétrécissait. Tandis que, 50 ans plus tôt, il avait fallu des semaines à la Grande-Bretagne pour être informée de la grande mutinerie indienne, les nouvelles faisaient à présent le tour du globe en quelques minutes. L'est et l'ouest se rejoignaient en des lieux et en des occasions invraisemblables. Les gens riaient et pleuraient, se réjouissaient ou plongeaient dans la dépression, aimaient ou haïssaient, dédaignaient le passé et se tournaient vers ce qu'ils croyaient être un avenir lumineux. Une nouvelle décennie ne faisait que passer.

Mysterious goings-on at a seance in Paris, c. 1900. Despite rapid
developments in technology, education and communication, the
1900s witnessed a revival of interest in all things occult.

Merkwürdiges Treiben bei einer spiritistischen Sitzung in Paris,
um 1900. Trotz des raschen Fortschritts der Technik, im Bildungs-
und Nachrichtenwesen lebte zu Beginn des 20. Jahrhunderts das
Interesse am Okkultismus wieder auf.

Événements étranges lors d'une séance de tables tournantes à
Paris, vers 1900. En dépit de l'évolution rapide des technologies,
de l'éducation et des communications, les années 1900 virent un
renouveau d'intérêt pour toutes les sciences occultes.

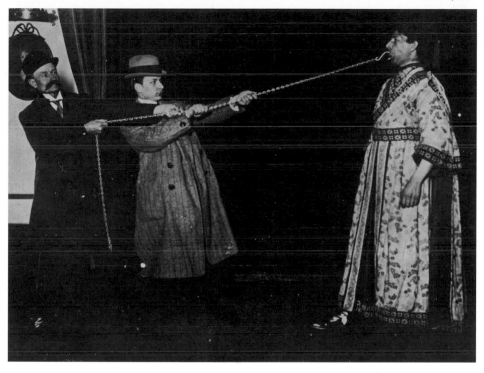

Don't try this at home. Almost anything bizarre found its way onto a theatrical stage. Here, two men engage in a tug of war with a third who has the end of the chain fastened to a hook through his lip. Sadly, we do not know what they did for an encore.

Versuchen Sie dies ja nicht zu Hause. Was merkwürdig genug war, kam auf eine Bühne. Hier machen zwei Männer ein Tauziehen mit einem dritten, bei dem das Ende einer Kette in der Lippe eingehakt ist. Leider wissen wir nicht, was es bei der Zugabe zu sehen gab.

Mieux vaut ne pas essayer ça chez soi ! Le bizarre, dans presque toutes ses occurrences, trouvait son expression dans les théâtres. Ici, deux hommes engagés dans une lutte déchaînée contre un homme qui tient l'autre extrémité accrochée à sa lèvre. L'histoire ne dit malheureusement pas ce qu'ils firent pour les rappels.

The wonders of civilisation. A German scientist poses by an Inca wall in Cuzco, Peru, c. 1900. The stones of the wall have been numbered so that it can be dismantled, carted off and rebuilt elsewhere.

Die Wunder der Zivilisation. Ein deutscher Wissenschaftler vor einer Inka-Mauer in Cuzco, Peru, um 1900. Die Steine der Mauer sind durch-nummeriert. So konnte man die Mauer abbauen, wegbringen und an einem anderen Ort wieder aufbauen.

Les merveilles de la civilisation. Un savant allemand posant devant le mur d'un édifice inca à Cuzco, Pérou, vers 1900. Les pierres de ce mur avaient été numérotées pour être descellées, démontées et remontées ailleurs.

The wonders of nature. Early 20th-century mountaineers cross a crevasse in the Alps, 1900. There were few places left in the world that bold amateurs were not prepared to explore.

Die Wunder der Natur. Bergsteiger zu Beginn des 20. Jahrhunderts durchqueren eine Gletscherspalte in den Alpen, 1900. Es gab nur noch wenig Orte in der Welt, deren Erkundung die mutigen Amateursportler scheuten.

Les merveilles de la nature. Des alpinistes du début du siècle franchissent une crevasse dans les Alpes, 1900. Il restait peu d'endroits dans le monde que des amateurs audacieux ne fussent prêts à explorer.

Short rest. Swans are removed from a stretch of the River
Thames near Henley to make way for the annual regatta,
1 June 1900. They appear to be used to the procedure.

Kurze Pause. Schwäne werden von einem Abschnitt der
Themse in der Nähe von Henley weggebracht, um die Bahn
für die jährliche Regatta frei zu machen, 1. Juni 1900.
Es sieht so aus, als würden sie diese Prozedur bereits kennen.

Repos transitoire. Des cygnes sont retirés d'un tronçon de
la Tamise près de Henley pour laisser la place à la régate
annuelle, 1ᵉʳ juin 1900. Les volatiles semblent habitués à
cette procédure.

Eternal rest. A flower-bedecked coffin reaches its final mooring after a journey by punt, 3 June 1903. Although it seems sadly romantic today, it may well have been the most practical way of getting the deceased from home to graveyard.

Ewige Ruhe. Ein mit Blumen geschmückter Sarg findet seine letzte Ruhe in der Nähe eines Anlegeplatzes nach einer Fahrt mit dem Stakkahn, 3. Juni 1903. Wenn dies auch nach trauriger Romantik aussehen mag, so war es wohl eher die praktischste Art und Weise, den Verstorbenen von seinem Heim zum Friedhof zu bringen.

Repos éternel. Un cercueil couvert de fleurs atteint son lieu d'amarrage définitif après un voyage sur le pont, 3 juin 1903. Même si cela paraît teinté d'un romantisme mélancolique, c'est vraisemblablement pour des raisons pratiques que l'on transportait ainsi le mort de sa maison au tombeau.

Muhammadan friars. Despite increasing persecution, the whirling dervishes continued to practise their religious ceremonies in 1905. The dance from which they took their name involved spinning round for 30 minutes, to achieve a trance-like state.

Mohammedanische Mönche. Trotz immer stärkerer Verfolgung praktizierten die wirbelnden Derwische ihre religiösen Bräuche im Jahre 1905. Bei dem Tanz, von dem sich ihr Name herleitet, mussten sie sich eine halbe Stunde lang drehen, um sich so in Trance zu versetzen.

Des moines musulmans. En dépit de persécutions croissantes, les derviches tourneurs continuaient à maintenir leurs pratiques cérémonielles en 1905. La danse à laquelle ils doivent leur nom comporte une trentaine de minutes de tours sur eux-mêmes pour atteindre un état de transe.

Carmelite nun. This photograph of a sister praying in her cell was taken by Boyer d'Agen in 1904. The Order forbade its members turning to face a camera, or indeed anyone from the outside world.

Eine Karmeliterin. Dieses Foto einer Ordensschwester, die in ihrer Klosterzelle betet, wurde 1904 von Boyer d'Agen aufgenommen. Der Orden untersagte seinen Mitgliedern, ihr Gesicht vor einer Kamera oder einem Vertreter der Außenwelt zu zeigen.

Une sœur carmélite. Cette photo d'une religieuse priant dans sa cellule fut prise par Boyer d'Agen en 1904. L'ordre des carmélites interdisait à ses membres de présenter leurs visages à l'appareil comme à quiconque du monde extérieur.

Buildings crumble,
fires break out and
rubberneckers
gather to stare in
the aftermath of
the San Francisco
earthquake of 1906.

Gebäude stürzen ein,
Feuer bricht aus.
Neugierige kommen
in Scharen herbei,
um sich die Auswir-
kungen des Erdbe-
bens in San Francisco
im Jahre 1906
anzusehen.

Des immeubles
s'effondrent, des
incendies se décla-
rent et des badauds
s'assemblent pour
contempler les
ruines, après le
tremblement de
terre de San Fran-
cisco, 1906.

As these two policemen attempt to escort an elderly lady across a London street, it would seem that one of the trio is having difficulty hearing what is being said. Even money says it's the sergeant on the right.

Diese beiden Polizisten versuchen, einer alten Dame über eine Straße in London zu helfen. Es scheint, dass einer der drei nicht ganz versteht, was gesagt wird. Man könnte meinen, dass es sich um den Polizisten auf der rechten Seite handelt.

Tandis que ces deux policiers s'efforcent d'aider une vieille dame à traverser la rue, il semble que l'un des protagonistes de la scène ait des difficultés d'audition. Et ce n'est pas la vieille dame …

In all their Victorian finery a group of ladies have a nice cuppa during an outing at Loughton, Essex, August 1908. No doubt high on the conversational agenda was the appalling decline in morals among the young.

Ganz im Stile der viktorianischen Zeit herausgeputzt, genehmigt sich eine Gruppe von Damen bei einem Ausflug nach Loughton, Essex, ein Tässchen Tee, August 1908. Es besteht kein Zweifel, dass sie über den entsetzlichen moralischen Verfall der Jugend schwatzen.

Un groupe de dames dans leurs atours victoriens prennent le thé au cours d'une sortie à Loughton, Essex, août 1908. Il ne fait pas de doute que l'un des sujets de conversation devait être l'affreux déclin de la moralité chez les jeunes gens.

After a hard day ruling a subcontinent of some 300 million people, all a chap
could do at the end of it was flop into a wicker chair, read the newly-arrived
six-week-old copy of *The Times* and have a pedicure, Indian-style.

Nach einem harten Arbeitstag, an dem man einen Subkontinent mit ungefähr
300 Millionen Menschen regiert hatte, ließ sich dieser Mann am Ende des
Tages in einen Korbstuhl fallen, las das gerade eingetroffene, sechs Wochen
alte Exemplar der *Times* und ließ sich auf indische Art die Füße pflegen.

Après une dure journée passée à gouverner un sous-continent peuplé de
quelques 300 millions d'habitants, il n'y avait rien d'autre à faire que de
s'écrouler dans un fauteuil en rotin pour lire un exemplaire du *Times* vieux de
six semaines et tout juste arrivé, tout en livrant ses pieds au pédicure indien.

Indian military representatives take tea on the terrace of the Houses of Parliament with the Unionist Chief Whip, Lord Valentia (centre), 1902. They were in England for the Coronation of Edward VII.

Indische Vertreter des Militärs beim Tee mit dem Führer der Unionisten, Lord Valentia (Mitte) auf der Terrasse des Houses of Parliament, 1902. Zur Krönungsfeier von Edward VII. waren sie nach England gereist.

Des représentants de l'armée indienne prenant le thé sur la terrasse du Parlement britannique avec Lord Valentina (au centre), chef de file du Parti unioniste, 1902. Ils se trouvaient en Angleterre pour le couronnement d'Édouard VII.

High-handed…
The impresario
Visser exhibits the
'celebrated dwarf'
named Beaufort
before the camera,
c. 1900.

Starke Hände …
Der Impressario
Visser zeigt den
„berühmten Zwerg"
namens Beaufort
vor der Kamera,
um 1900.

Avoir le bras long …
L'imprésario Visser
exhibe le « célèbre
nain » Beaufort
devant l'appareil
photo, vers 1900.

Long-legged…
Possibly the tallest
woman in Britain
arrives in London,
26 May 1907.
She was booked
to appear at the
Hippodrome.

Große Füße …
Die wahrscheinlich
größte Frau in
Großbritannien
kommt in London
an, 26. Mai 1907.
Sie war für einen
Auftritt im
Hippodrome
gebucht worden.

… ou des jambes
plus longues …
Cette femme,
peut-être la plus
grande de toute la
Grande-Bretagne,
débarque à Londres
le 26 mai 1907.
Elle était invitée
à se produire à
l'hippodrome.

It required a mixture of ingenuity, patience and exploitation on the part of trainers to produce a team of football-playing dogs in June 1908. Whether the public was impressed is not known, but the scene has a 'backyard' look to it.

Eine Mischung aus Geschicklichkeit und Geduld sowie ein gewisses Maß an Ausbeutung waren seitens der Abrichter nötig, um eine Mannschaft von Fußball spielenden Hunden aufzustellen, Juni 1908. Ob das Publikum davon beeindruckt war, sei an dieser Stelle dahin gestellt. Es sieht jedoch eher nach einem Hinterhof aus.

Il fallait tout un mélange d'ingénuité, de patience et de tyrannie de la part des entraîneurs pour entraîner une équipe de chiens à jouer au football, juin 1908. On ignore si le public fut impressionné, mais la scène comporte un petit air d'arrière-cour.

Less enjoyable, from the animal's point of view, was the life of this dancing bear in London, c. 1900. The poor creature spent its nights in confinement and its days padding the city streets, earning its owner a living.

Weniger schön – aus der Sicht eines Tieres – war das Leben dieses Tanzbären in London, um 1900. Diese arme Kreatur verbrachte ihre Nächte in Gefangenschaft, und am Tage musste sie durch die Straßen der Stadt trotten, um den Lebensunterhalt ihres Besitzers zu verdienen.

Moins drôle était la vie de cet ours danseur à Londres, vers 1900. Le pauvre animal passait ses nuits en captivité et ses journées à amuser les passants dans les rues de la ville, pour faire vivre son maître.

Paris, 1900. Framed by the girders of the 12-year-old Eiffel Tower
is the Trocadero, centre-piece of the Paris Exhibition on the
Quai d'Orsay. It was Europe's biggest fair, covering 547 acres
(220 hectares).

Paris, 1900. Die Pfeiler des 12 Jahre alten Eiffelturmes umrahmen
hier das Trocadero, Mittelpunkt der Pariser Weltausstellung am Quai
d'Orsay. Mit 220 Hektar war es die größte Ausstellung in Europa.

Paris, 1900. Dans l'encadrement des poutrelles de la Tour Eiffel,
vieille d'à peine 12 ans, apparaît le Trocadéro, pièce maîtresse de
l'Exposition de Paris sur le Quai d'Orsay. Cette foire, la plus grande
d'Europe, couvrait 220 hectares de terrain.

London, 1908. Reinhold Thiele's reflective study of the Indian-style Court of Honour at the Anglo-French Exhibition at the White City. Later the same year, a part of the site was the setting for the Olympic Games.

London, 1908. Reinhold Thieles reflektive Aufnahme des britischen im indischen Stil gehaltenen Court of Honour auf der englisch-französischen Ausstellung in White City. Einige Zeit später im selben Jahr wurde ein Teil dieser Anlage zum Schauplatz der Olympischen Spiele.

Londres, 1908. Étude par Reinhold Thiele des reflets de la Cour d'honneur de style indien à l'Exposition anglo-française de White City. Quelques mois plus tard, une partie de ce site fournit le cadre des Jeux olympiques.

The old, the frail and possibly the lazy travel to the Paris International Exhibition of 1900 by Bath-Chair. For the porters it was perhaps as well that the Exhibition was held in the city centre.

Die alten, schwachen und möglicherweise auch die faulen Leute fahren in Rollstühlen zur Pariser Weltausstellung im Jahre 1900. Für die schiebenden Dienstmänner war es nur von Vorteil, dass sich die Ausstellung im Stadtzentrum befand.

Des personnes âgées, fragiles ou simplement paresseuses se rendent à l'Exposition universelle en fauteuil roulant, Paris, 1900. Pour les porteurs, il était peut-être tout aussi bien que l'exposition ait lieu au cœur de la ville.

A view down Eyre Street Hill in the City of London, 1907. At the time it was London's version of Little Italy, the home of the Italian community. Today it is fashionable Clerkenwell, though still a very Italian part of London.

Ein Blick entlang der Eyre Street Hill im Zentrum von London, 1907. Zu jener Zeit war dies Londons Variante von Little Italy, dem Zuhause der italienischen Gemeinde. Heute befindet sich hier das vornehme Clerkenwell. Das Flair dieses Stadtteils ist noch immer sehr italienisch.

Une vue de Eyre Street Hill, dans la City de Londres, 1907. À l'époque, c'était la version londonienne de Little Italy, le cœur de la communauté italienne. Aujourd'hui, c'est Clerkenwell, un quartier à la mode et toujours très italien.

The scene is a
Midlands street.
The theme is
eternal. The
costumes are
those of 1904.
Boy and girl step
out on a Bank
Holiday morning.

Eine Straße in den
Midlands. Das
Motiv ist zeitlos.
Die Kleidung
stammt aus dem
Jahr 1904. Am
Morgen eines
Feiertags spaziert
ein junges Paar
diese Straße entlang.

La scène se passe
dans une rue des
Midlands. Le thème
en est éternel. Les
costumes sont de
1904. Des amou-
reux sortent par un
matin de jour férié.

Index

gettyimages

Over 70 million images and 30,000 hours of film footage are held by the various collections owned by Getty Images. These cover a vast number of subjects from the earliest photojournalism to current press photography, sports, social history and geography. Getty Images' conceptual imagery is renowned amongst creative end users.

www.gettyimages.com

Über 70 Millionen Bilder und 30 000 Stunden Film befinden sich in den verschiedenen Archiven von Getty Images. Sie decken ein breites Spektrum an Themen ab – von den ersten Tagen des Fotojournalismus bis hin zu aktueller Pressefotografie, Sport, Sozialgeschichte und Geographie. Bei kreativen Anwendern ist das Material von Getty Images für seine ausdrucksstarke Bildsprache bekannt.

www.gettyimages.com

Plus de 70 millions d'images et 30 000 heures de films sont détenus par les différentes collections dont Getty Images est le propriétaire. Cela couvre un nombre considérable de sujets – des débuts du photojournalisme aux photographies actuelles de presse, de sport, d'histoire sociale et de géographie. Le concept photographique de Getty Images est reconnu des créatifs.

www.gettyimages.com